The Online Broker and Trading Directory

Larry Chambers
with Karen Johnson

McGraw-Hill

NEW YORK   SAN FRANCISCO   WASHINGTON, D.C.   AUCKLAND   BOGOTÁ
CARACAS   LISBON   LONDON   MADRID   MEXICO CITY   MILAN
MONTREAL   NEW DELHI   SAN JUAN   SINGAPORE
SYDNEY   TOKYO   TORONTO

McGraw-Hill

A Division of The McGraw·Hill Companies

1 2 3 4 5 6 7 8 9 0 DOC/DOC 9 0 9 8 7 6 5 4 3 2 1 0 9

ISBN 0-07-135425-5

The sponsoring editor for this book was Stephen Isaacs, the editing supervisor was Janice Race, and the production supervisor was Elizabeth J. Strange. It was set in Giovanni by North Market Street Graphics.

Printed and bound by R. R. Donnelley & Sons Company.

This publication is designed to provide accurate and authoritative information in regard to the subject matter covered. It is sold with the understanding that neither the author nor the publisher is engaged in rendering legal, accounting, or other professional service. If legal advice or other expert assistance is required, the services of a competent professional person should be sought.
> —*From a Declaration of Principles jointly adopted by a Committee of the American Bar Association and a Committee of Publishers.*

McGraw-Hill books are available at special quantity discounts to use as premiums and sales promotions, or for use in corporate training programs. For more information, please write to the Director of Special Sales, McGraw-Hill, 11 West 19th Street, New York, NY 10011. Or contact your local bookstore.

 This book is printed on recycled, acid-free paper containing a minimum of 50% recycled de-inked fiber

Library of Congress Cataloging-in-Publication Data
Chambers, Larry.
    The online broker and trading directory / by Larry Chambers
    with Karen Johnson.
      p.   cm.
    ISBN 0-07-135425-5
    1. Investments—Computer network resources Directories. 2. Web sites Directories. 3. Electronic trading of securities.   I. Title.
HG4515.95.C48   1999
025.06'3326—dc21
                                             99-37786
                                               CIP

Contents

Acknowledgments   *iv*

Part 1   **Tools and Rules to Get You Started**   1
             Direct Access Has Arrived!   3
             Introduction to Electronic Trading   6
             Getting Connected   19
             Tips for Selecting an Online Broker   24
             Choosing the Right Order   27
             Useful Abbreviations   28

Part 2   **Online Trading Sites**   31
             DISCOUNT ONLINE TRADING SITES   33
             LEVEL II TRADING SITES   151
             DIRECT ACCESS TRADING SITES   199
             SPECIALTY SITES   235

             Conclusion   *250*

Acknowledgments

My thanks and appreciation extend to: Karen Johnson, my significant other and partner, who spent countless hours checking and rechecking trading sites and learning the lingo.

Stephen Isaacs, my editor at McGraw-Hill; Charles "Chip" Roame, managing principal of the Tiburon Strategic Advisors, LLC; and David Nassar, author of *The Electronic Day Trader* and president of Market Wise Trading, whose insightful book answered many questions.

John Aidan Byrne, editor at *Traders Magazine*, and Ed Gorman, at Reynders Gray & Co., who provided an up-close-and-personal experience at the New York Stock Exchange.

Part 1

Tools and Rules to Get You Started

DIRECT ACCESS HAS ARRIVED!

Maybe you're already a seasoned online trader, or you've been using a discount broker without satisfactory results, or you just want to take a look at what everybody is talking about over lunch or coffee. This directory will familiarize you with the differences, and the similarities, of more than 100 online trading sites. It can help you if you're a novice or an active trader or have experience trading and simply want to learn more about online investing. Tap into the after-hours stock market or choose your avenue of execution. Save time and money, discover the full price of a trade, and more.

The introduction (Part 1) will familiarize you with the online brokerage environment, explain how markets work (including the difference between Nasdaq and the New York Stock Exchange), offer information on valuable investment tools such as software requirements and Internet connections, and review key criteria for selecting an online broker.

Part 2 is the core of this directory. Here online traders can discover the best sites for active trading and pinpoint sites that offer the after-hours market or specialty trades. This part segregates Web trading sites by the level of functionality they currently provide:

- Discount Online Trading Sites—for the intermediate-term to long-term investor.
- Level II Trading Sites—provide access to real-time data for a broader range of trades and accounts.
- Direct Access Trading Sites—for the day trader, including after-hours sites, a new venue for active traders.
- Specialty Sites—for investors who are particularly interested in bonds, options, futures, and foreign markets.

In assembling this book, we began by reviewing over 200 sites and quickly found that many were just online sales brochures, specialty sites, or sites for professionals and institutions. While dozens of sites offered everything from news reports to detailed financial analysis of individual stocks, they did not accommodate trading. The Web is a proliferation of names with subscription services linked together. We boiled this number down to approximately 100 real trading sites, recognizing that half of those are simply order routing systems, or e-mail order messenger systems.

There is a wide discrepancy in fees for the same services from site to site. Many of the active trading sites are more costly at first glance, but after reviewing the features and order entry methods, you'll soon discover who presents value. Many sites promote loss leaders by offering free or nearly free trades, but the bargain is for a type of trade you seldom make, or there's a shopping list of add-on fees that puts your total cost right back in the ballpark with the other sites. It's a little like buying a computer from a mail-order house only to discover when it arrives that the monitor was not included in the price. So while it would be easy on the eyes to have just one commission per site for comparison, there are many variables that you have to consider. Some sites price their trades by ticket, others by shares, still others "tier" commissions on the basis of monthly volume. To complicate matters, the exchange and ECN fees change from site to site.

Many of the sites were encumbered with link advertisements, some were fun to navigate, others were organized with excellent information—but my goal was not to rate looks, navigation, or size. We have pulled out only the comparative information that will prove pertinent to your trading decisions. So when you review a site, there's no sales hype or flashing, spinning signs, just basic information that can save you time—and money!

Where do you begin? First, you'll need to determine your personal trading style and goals. Before you can compare data from one site to another, you'll need to understand how you intend to trade, how much, and how often. Be sure to check the minimum account balance (under Fees) before going with any site. The type and amount of stock quotes and information you need will vary according to your trading experience and desire for broker guidance or trade assistance. If you plan to daytrade, or hold your positions only minutes, you'll be looking for speed and price and possibly want to direct your trades' execution. Longerterm traders may be more interested in the research provided.

You will discover that the availability of sites depends on what kind of hardware and software you're willing to pay for. If you're just starting out, nothing is going to be more upsetting than to open up an account and find out that your computer system is out of date, or that the appealing feature of the site requires software with costly monthly fees attached.

As you move through this directory, take time out to visit a few of the actual trading sites. Some sites grow and develop; some change addresses; some close down as new ones open. Keep this book next to your computer or in the top drawer of your desk. By having the book handy, you won't have to wait for a Web search query or rummage through your notes, or worse, waste time moving from site to site. Find what you want, then go directly there.

To make your job easier, each site profile is broken down in the following manner:

NAME OF PROVIDER

URL: Web address. Also appears at the top of each directory page.

TYPE OF SITE: A quick overview of the site's mission—for example, to provide integrated financial services online.

USERS: The types of traders who will most benefit from the site.

SNAIL MAIL: Postal address of headquarters, generally for receiving account application/signature forms.

PHONE: Toll-free number when available.

E-MAIL: Generally for customer service.

SERVICES: Key elements or features of the site, including a description of data, trading systems, types of trades, and other services that the site offers.

EXECUTION SYSTEMS: The site's order entry and execution process, including the clearing agency—the company that routes the order to the appropriate exchange or market.

FEES: Minimum account requirements, quote data and software fees, and range of transaction fees (including add-ons).

APPEALING FEATURES: The most intriguing or practical features of this site.

SUPPORT SYSTEMS: Technical and trading support contact information; software installation/use and trading education offered; outside resources, site guides, and how to open an account.

OPERATIONAL SYSTEMS: Hardware and software requirements, operating systems, modem speed, and connectivity.

BACKGROUND INFORMATION: Notable facts about the site provider.

INTRODUCTION TO ELECTRONIC TRADING

High technology in the financial services industry used to be an electronic message board flashing trades a few minutes after they happened. Quotron machines sat on mahogany credenzas, and the Dow Jones news service tapped out news a day before it reached the *Wall Street Journal*. It used to take weeks before the earnings were translated into analysts' reports, which were then mailed to investors. Clients had to call a stockbroker to obtain quotes and to buy or sell a stock. Commissions on the same transaction ranged between $100 and $450, depending on the firm. Several hours after a trade, a client received a verbal confirmation, and a week later the investor was sent a written statement.

Today, virtually any investor with a computer gets earnings reports in real time—the moment they're completed. If you want a current stock price, it's only a few keystrokes away. To trade, you have several options. You can still call your broker, or you can do it yourself at a choice of levels and even direct your trade's routing. You can watch your order being executed, or receive a trade confirmation in a matter of minutes. You will be alerted to price fluctuations by e-mail or pager. Until recently, all you needed was a computer with a modem. Now, as soon as you have a trading account, you can punch in a trade on your touch-tone telephone or personal digital assistant (PDA).

Costly trading commissions continue to shrink to a single digit as brokerages fight to attract your account. In fact, trading costs seem as if they are diving toward free. The war for customers between online brokers and full service firms will keep driving trading costs even lower. The discount brokers have done a terrific job of adapting and moving largely onto the Web.

Just a few years ago, online stock trading was nothing more than "cybercuriosity," which now has exploded into popularity. Last year, according to Credit Suisse/First Boston, the number of Americans investing over the Internet grew 120%. Online trading now accounts for every seventh retail stock trade. Schwab reports that 2.2 million accounts—almost 70% of its trades, 100,000 transactions a day—are coming via the Web. It is estimated that there are more than 7 million online investing accounts, representing 20% of all brokerage accounts, and that percentage is expected to double in two years.

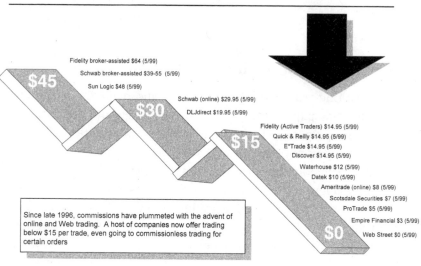

Commissions Are Rapidly Heading Toward Zero

$45

Fidelity broker-assisted $64 (5/99)
Schwab broker-assisted $39-55 (5/99)
Sun Logic $48 (5/99)

$30

Schwab (online) $29.95 (5/99)
DLJdirect $19.95 (5/99)

$15

Fidelity (Active Traders) $14.95 (5/99)
Quick & Reilly $14.95 (5/99)
E*Trade $14.95 (5/99)
Discover $14.95 (5/99)
Waterhouse $12 (5/99)
Datek $10 (5/99)
Ameritrade (online) $8 (5/99)
Scotsdale Securities $7 (5/99)
ProTrade $5 (5/99)
Empire Financial $3 (5/99)
Web Street $0 (5/99)

$0

Since late 1996, commissions have plummeted with the advent of online and Web trading. A host of companies now offer trading below $15 per trade, even going to commissionless trading for certain orders

Note: Many firms have qualifiers on their low prices. For instance, at E*Trade you pay an additional $15 ($34.95) for a broker-assisted and $.01 per share for all shares on orders over 5000 shares. Waterhouse has the same $.01 charge per share on large orders; Accutrade is $29.95 for up to 1000 shares and then $29.95 plus $.02/share. Web Street is at $0 over 1000 shares valued at $2 or more.

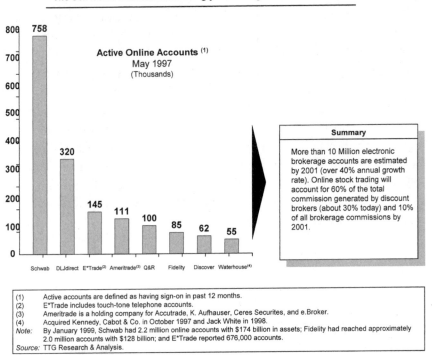

The Self-Serve Market Is Increasingly Becoming an Online Game

Active Online Accounts [1]
May 1997
(Thousands)

- Schwab: 758
- DLJdirect: 320
- E*Trade [2]: 145
- Ameritrade [3]: 111
- Q&R: 100
- Fidelity: 85
- Discover: 62
- Waterhouse [4]: 55

Summary

More than 10 Million electronic brokerage accounts are estimated by 2001 (over 40% annual growth rate). Online stock trading will account for 60% of the total commission generated by discount brokers (about 30% today) and 10% of all brokerage commissions by 2001.

(1)	Active accounts are defined as having sign-on in past 12 months.
(2)	E*Trade includes touch-tone telephone accounts.
(3)	Ameritrade is a holding company for Accutrade, K. Aufhauser, Ceres Securites, and e.Broker.
(4)	Acquired Kennedy, Cabot & Co. in October 1997 and Jack White in 1998.
Note:	By January 1999, Schwab had 2.2 million online accounts with $174 billion in assets; Fidelity had reached approximately 2.0 million accounts with $128 billion; and E*Trade reported 676,000 accounts.
Source:	TTG Research & Analysis.

Where Do You Go Online?

Online investing articles fill the magazines and make the headlines of every major newspaper's front page. The challenge, and the purpose of this book, is to figure out how to use all that information effectively. Where do you go online to buy and sell stocks, get trading information or research? There are hundreds of sites offering everything from companies' annual reports to detailed financial analyses of individual stocks, but not all of them accommodate trading. Search engines help you find sites quickly by simply entering the URL (online site address). Once you're in, you have to learn how to navigate the site for the information you desire. Throughout this directory you'll find the basic information you need without the sales literature woven around it.

If you decide to buy a stock, the next step is to find a site that you feel comfortable with—one that's easy to navigate, with services that meet your objectives. That's where looking through this book can save you time.

Once you've selected a site and opened your account, what do you do? You can type in your stock ticker symbol—the market abbreviation used for buying and selling stocks or mutual funds through an exchange. If you don't know the symbol, most sites, search engines, or news services have a window called Symbol Lookup. Click on it, type in the name of the company you want, and instantly get the symbol. If you want to know the symbol for Yahoo, for example, you click on the Symbol Lookup box and type in Yahoo. The Yahoo Inc. symbol turns out to be YHOO. Click on the symbol. The next screen to appear will give you a detailed look at YHOO's daily trading activity, including the number of shares that have exchanged hands that day, last price, average high and low, normal trading volume, 52-week high and low, company's earnings per share, price-to-earnings ratio, dividends and dividend yield, along with a chart that can be modified to show short- and long-term trading trends. This is called a Level I screen.

Sites also have news icons that you can click on to bring up recent headlines. You can click on Research to get an analyst's comments and ratings. Analysts rate the companies on a scale of 1 to 5, with 1 equaling a strong buy and 5 equaling a strong sell. There is also a series of charts and screens showing how many analysts are recommending the stock as a *strong buy*, a *buy*, a *hold*, or a *sell*.

If you hit your Back (arrow) icon, you can return to the previous page to select another option called Profile. This takes you to a page that includes a brief company description, the name of the top executives, and any pertinent earnings or cashflow data in a lineup with links labeled Company News, History, Latest Stock Price, SEC Filing, Investor Relations, and the message board. A word of caution: Don't put too much store in message boards. They are the equivalent of electronic chat rooms.

As you become more informed, you grow more confident in managing your own stock portfolio. Still, there are snags that come with the growth and popularity—duplicate trades, investors getting misprices, site computers going down, and more. Many serious online traders have accounts at more than one online brokerage company so that if one site goes down they have an alternative.

The sites profiled in this directory fall into many different market segments, from so-called full service firms, such as Charles Schwab and

Waterhouse Securities—which also offer local branch offices and a full range of products—to firms like E*Trade and Ameritrade that don't offer any branch offices. Plus, there are many low-cost sites such as Datek Online and SureTrade. At the time of this publication, the Wall Street firms are just getting their acts together. Most traditional Wall Street firms regarded online trading as a curiosity or small niche when it first appeared in 1994, but the game is changing rapidly.

Just as the research for this book was submitted for publication, Merrill Lynch & Co. made a complete about-face and adopted a new business model, offering online trading at a price to compete with its low-cost trading rivals. Just a year ago, Merrill executives scoffed at cyberinvesting. Merrill is the nation's largest brokerage house. When the biggest enters the game, the rest have to follow. Merrill's turnabout also demonstrates how profoundly the Internet is transforming the competitive landscape.

Merrill Lynch will charge $29.95 per trade for trades up to 1000 shares. The site name is ML Direct. It will also offer an unlimited number of free trades for an annual minimum fee of $1500. Investors can enter orders with a broker, online, or by touch-tone phone. Merrill is a powerhouse in research, underwriting, mergers and acquisitions, and asset management. What can the average online brokerage offer to compete?

Online vs. Day Trading

The majority of online trading sites do little more than take orders and route them to a third party for execution. The sites may have spinning golden dollar signs and links to news services, but they offer only bare-bones tools. Those sites that are comprehensive in their services are swamped with users. There's still plenty of room for sophisticated players like Merrill Lynch and Prudential. The differentiating factor in today's online trading world is direct access to streaming, real-time data, quotes, and order entry. This is what separates the day traders from the online traders. There seems to be an enormous amount of confusion in the media around the basic differences between these two concepts: online trading and day trading.

ONLINE TRADERS: Online trading is simply investing using the tools of the Internet. This can be short- to long-term investing. You can use technical or fundamental analysis, or a combination of the two. You may carry your position for a day to many years. You have access to all the markets on the Internet or dial-up or through proprietary software controlled by your brokerage firm, and the speed of execution is within minutes.

Online traders may be do-it-yourself investors or experienced traders. They are already using the Internet to enter orders, make switches, and improve stock positions. They typically make 25 trades a year—about two a month. That's still considered investing, not day trading. These investors want to see who offers better services at lower costs, or take a test drive of the system before making that next trade.

Newcomers to online trading may have never bought a stock from a broker, advisor, or financial planner in their life. They just want to get started investing or have the opportunity to personally direct their IRA and make changes inside their 401(k) plans. Many feel like they're missing something because everywhere they look, the hot topic is online trading.

DAY TRADERS: Day traders capitalize on small movements of stocks on an intraday basis, often ignoring fundamental analysis of the underlying securities. Their time frame for holding a security is usually minutes, with no overnight position. The speed of execution is within seconds. They access the market with Nasdaq Level II information, by way of a broker-dealer, using high-speed T1 connections with ISDN backup. Day trading is a high-risk activity that should be engaged in only by those who fully understand the techniques and the risks.

Most day traders fall into one of two camps. The *scalpers* rely heavily on riding the market momentum as short-term traders who buy and sell throughout the day in order to profit from small, fractional price changes in a security. Scalpers contribute greatly to the liquidity of the market. In the next camp are the *position traders*—an all-encompassing category for traders who use various technical guides, such as real-time charts with technical studies. They generally hold a position longer than scalpers, but still "go flat" at the end of the day.

Either way, day traders are dependent on the visual capability of streaming quote screens and charts, on seeing real-time executions, and on viewing the last trade and volume that was executed. All of this comes from state-of-the-art software and technology.

How do online trading and day trading work with the various markets?

The NYSE

The New York Stock Exchange is an *agency* auction market. What does that really mean and what are the advantages? The essential point is that trading at the NYSE takes place by open bids and offers by exchange members, acting as agents for institutions or individual investors. Buy and sell orders meet directly on the trading floor, and prices are determined by the interplay of supply and demand. In contrast, in the over-the-counter (OTC) market, the price is determined by a dealer who buys and sells out of inventory.

At the NYSE, each listed stock is assigned to a single post where the specialist manages the auction process. NYSE members bring all orders for NYSE-listed stocks to the exchange floor either electronically or physically by a floor broker. As a result, the flow of buy and sell orders for each stock is funneled to a single location. This heavy stream of diverse orders provides liquidity—the ease with which securities can be bought and sold without wide price fluctuations.

The trading floor is still where all NYSE transactions occur. It is a 36,000-square-foot facility designed specifically to support the centralized auction. It is where market professionals, supported by advanced technology, represent the orders of buyers and sellers to determine prices according to the laws of supply and demand.

The trading floor houses 17 trading posts, each staffed by specialists and specialist clerks. Every listed security is traded in a unique location at one of these posts and by one specialist, thus ensuring that all trading interest is centralized. All buying and selling takes place around these posts. Computer monitors above each specialist location show which stocks are traded there.

After the order has been completed in the auction market, a report of execution is returned directly to the member firm office, over the same electronic circuit that brought the order to the trading floor. SuperDOT (designated order turnaround)—the NYSE's electronic order routing system—can currently process about 25 billion shares per day.

There are approximately 1500 trading booths along the perimeter of the trading floor where brokers obtain orders. Orders are transmitted to broker booth locations from off the floor either by telephone or electronically through the Broker Booth Support System (BBSS). Once an

---

TRADING ON THE NYSE

THE TRADER enters an order through an online broker.

THE BROKER either electronically sends the order to a "specialist" operating on the exchange floor or routes it to a floor broker at the exchange, who physically walks the order over to the trading area.

THE MARKET SPECIALIST consolidates the order with all others, then announces the best available price as well as the number of shares available at that price.

THE FLOOR BROKER makes a bid for the stock on the basis of that price, competing with other brokers assembled in the trading area.

THE SPECIALIST AWARDS the stock to successful bidders. If no buyers appear, the specialist is required by the NYSE to be buyer of last resort. In exchange for providing liquidity in the stock, the specialist is allowed to profit from the price differential of stocks he or she buys during price declines, then sells as the price rises.

---

order is received, the broker represents that order as an agent in the trading crowd of that stock.

BBSS allows member firms to selectively route orders electronically to either the trading post or the booths on the NYSE trading floor. BBSS electronically supports the following broker functions: receiving orders, entering orders, rerouting orders, issuing reports, conducting research, and viewing other services via terminal "windows."

The Nasdaq

Unlike the NYSE, the Nasdaq (National Association of Security Dealers Automated Quotation) system is not a physical exchange. Rather, it is composed of a network of thousands of dealers who are connected electronically. The Nasdaq market relies on individual market makers rather than a single specialist to provide liquidity in over-the-counter (OTC) securities. These market makers combine their efforts in each stock to collectively provide a market. This is referred to as honoring the two-sided market. Essentially, if market makers are willing to sell a stock at one price, there must be a reasonable price at which they are willing to

---

TRADING ON THE NASDAQ

THE TRADER enters an order through an online broker.

THE BROKER transmits the order to a single market maker (a Nasdaq-sanctioned trader providing a market for the stock), who fills the order from his or her own inventory, or routes the order through SelectNet or one of several electronic communications networks (ECNs), where it can be seen by everyone with access to those networks. Competing market makers can then act on the order.

THE MARKET MAKER may sell the trader the stock at the ask price, then turn around and initiate a new lower bid to buy the stock back at a lower price. In this way the market maker profits from the spread between the bid and ask price.

---

buy. The average investor sees only the best bid or offer (NBBO, national best bid and offer). Orders can be executed instantaneously.

SelectNet

NASD provides the SelectNet System, an electronic order-routing system that is the counterpart of the NYSE's SuperDot. It is a negotiation tool that allows market makers to communicate with each other electronically and privately. Here, market makers can bid or offer a stock to another market maker without having to make a phone call or show quotes publicly.

Electronic Communications Networks (ECNs)

ECNs are private communications networks that allow public investors to broadcast prices on the Nasdaq. The system gives traders the ability to bypass a market maker and buy or sell directly with other traders. ECNs work as order matching systems, and allow traders to advertise a price sometimes better than the current bid or offer.

Two years ago, 75% of trades were executed on SOES (small order execution systems) on the Nasdaq. SOES, Nasdaq's automatic order execution system, is designed to favor small public market and executable limit orders. SOES automatically matches and executes orders, locks in a price, and sends confirmation directly to the broker-dealers on both sides of the trade. Institutions and broker-dealers may not employ SOES to trade for their own accounts.

Today, less than 5% of trades are on SOES. Instead, trades are being executed on the ECNs: Instinet (INCA), Bloomberg's Trade Book (BTRD), Island (ISLD), Spear Leeds (REDI), and Brass (BRUT)—to name a few. There are about nine major ECNs out there, and quite often they quote better prices than the Nasdaq. True, you pay a premium for utilizing an ECN, but the price improvement that you get on 1000 shares more than offsets that premium.

Let's say you're going to buy 1000 shares of XXB. On 1000 shares, a one-eighth point price improvement is worth $125. If you could improve the price—that is, get a better price than the $125 on an ECN than you could on the Nasdaq—even if you had to pay $20 more for that execution, you'd still be $105 ahead.

Now, let's turn that around. Say you've bought XXB and now want to sell it, so you go looking for a bid. You find that the Nasdaq bids are $20\frac{3}{8}$ to $20\frac{5}{8}$. It looks like you could make a profit, but you flash over the ECNs and discover a better bid on the Instinet at $20\frac{1}{2}$. It would be better to sell on the Instinet bid than the Nasdaq bid.

The granddaddy of the ECNs is still Instinet (INCA). Instinet is a system that was set up to allow the big institutions to bargain with each other. Instinet allows a mechanism for the two to come together on a price anonymously. It's still used for that. The top 100 stocks in terms of volume on the Nasdaq are trading up to 50% of their volume on the ECNs, not the Nasdaq. And the ECNs make up over 25% of Nasdaq's total daily volume. It's huge and it's growing—and it is an enormous source of competition for the Nasdaq.

So how does the online broker make any money?

Payment for Order Flow

One way is by selling trades to a wholesale broker-dealer. In exchange for getting that order flow, the wholesaler pays the brokerage for the order.

Say you want to buy 1000 shares at $20 a share on your favorite trading site. The site broker sells the unfilled order to a wholesaler, which in turn clones that price—knowing that it's the number you, back home, are looking at on your computer screen. The wholesaler fills your order at 20¼ and buys those shares on the Instinet at 20⅛. The dealer just traded ahead of your order. The wholesaler made money, plus paid $.02 per share to the retailer (site broker) for sending along the order.

That's the difference. If you're going to buy a security and hold it for six months, are you really concerned about a one-eighth improvement? You probably want an easy way to launch your order, buy your stock, and hope it goes up in six months. But if you don't want to be "long"— in the market—overnight, it becomes very difficult to take advantage of rapid movements and intramarket imbalances. You're going to need a site that offers different *levels* of information.

Quote Levels

Nasdaq provides several levels of quotes that disseminate differing amounts of information to the user. An Internet system generally gives the user a Level I quote, and that's what you'll find at most of the sites. Level I quotes display the inside bid and offer prices as well as the number of market makers willing to buy and sell at those prices.

Because of normal market price fluctuations, as well as the speed of the Internet, a Level I quote as it appears on the screen may or may not be accurate. A broker cannot guarantee a Level I price to a customer. Most Internet and subscription-based quote services provide this information on a delayed basis. When price quotations are delayed, the subscribing site isn't paying the exchange fee. When the quotes are live, or streaming, a fee is required—which adds to the monthly cost by the user.

For example, a typical Level I quote might read XYZ 128¼ × 128⅜. This quote provides you with the basic information necessary to see what range the stock is trading at, and for investors who make only one or two trades in a month or a year, it will be sufficient. But a Level I quote is fundamentally inadequate for gauging real market makers' interest in the stock. First of all, it doesn't tell you who is bidding or offering stock. You would have no way of knowing how much stock each market maker is advertising to buy or sell. There could be one market maker on the bid willing to buy 1000 shares and another offering to sell 100 shares. A trader looking at Level I quotes will not be able to determine which market makers are willing to buy and which are willing to sell.

Fortunately, the Nasdaq has another quote option that shows not only the number of market makers on the bid and offer but also the amount that they are advertising to buy or sell as well as the actual names of the market makers. Level II, until recently, was available only to professional trading desks and brokerage firms. It's now available on several of the sites.

Only recently has the public been allowed to access it. The true value in real-time Level II data is that it allows you to choose your avenue of execution. This Level II quote is an invaluable tool for gauging the strength and size of a stock as well as finding out who the key players are. The same quote as above shown on a Level II screen may look more like this: XYZ 10 128¼; GSCO × 1; 128⅜ MSCO 1; 128⅜ SALB 1; 128⅜ MLCO 1; 128⅜ PRUS. Seeing a Level II screen and all the market makers on both sides of the market indicating price and volume makes the market transparent.

The reason you're not going to find Level II screens on most of the sites is cost. The Nasdaq charges a fee, and that becomes the premium charged to the trader for the advantage of viewing the behind-the-scenes information. Many sites are now offering links to independent subscription quotation databases, which users can employ at their option.

Many online traders just want to buy a security or two on their own without their broker's involvement. They are looking for an easy way to launch their orders, observe their picks, and monitor their positions until a profit can be taken. On the other hand, if you are looking for the imbalances in the *bid* and the *ask* prices among all these electronic communications networks, you need to have an ongoing investigation of who offers what and for how much.

Trade with the Pros

Imagine a trading system that will eliminate the need for market makers and specialists! Some direct access online sites and extended hours trading platforms are now allowing individual investors to represent themselves, viewing the Order Book and tracking an order from entry to execution in real time the same way professional traders do. Currently, People's Stock Network buyers and sellers can already trade 19 issues without the aid of a broker.

Institutions break up their orders into little pieces, then trade them at varying prices, thus anonymously buying or selling large blocks of stock without news of a transaction leaking into the market and causing prices to move before their trade closes. OptiMark Technologies new system, in development for four years with the Pacific Exchange, now has an algorithm that will do the same thing for retail investors. Launched in January 1999, the system is expected eventually to also allow traders to buy and sell shares of the NYSE and AMEX. OptiMark's backers include Goldman, Sachs & Co. and other investment banks, plus 15-percent owner Dow Jones & Co.

One of the last barriers that has kept the investment public on the outside of the world of the stock analysts are their conference calls. These are private phone calls between company insiders and analysts and portfolio managers. Yahoo!, Microsoft, Intel, and Sun Microsystems have already been letting investors click into their calls. Nasdaq has launched a pilot program with Broadcast.com to Webcast their conference calls (11 of the Nasdaq 100 companies are participating). Some of the sites that offer conference calls are:

- Bestcalls.com (www.bestcalls.com)—corporate earnings; news; provides e-mail reminders of calls.
- Broadcast.com (www.broadcast.com)—to find a conference call schedule, go to the "business" channel and click on "companies."
- Streetfusion (www.streetfusion.com)—formerly c-call.com, for Wall Street pros; very active site; more than 600 calls.
- VCall (www.vcall.com)—broadcasts earnings and other news events of more than 350 public companies.

Why Extended Hours Trading?

For years, institutional and professional investors have been able to trade around the clock, in real time, whether the exchanges are open or not, while the individual investor's options have been very limited or nonexistent.

The major stock exchanges close at 4 pm Eastern time. If you enter orders online after the exchanges close, your orders aren't executed until the market reopens the next day. In contrast, extended hours trading lets you invest with greater convenience, with the benefit of reacting to developing news, after-market announcements, etc., just like the institutions and professionals do.

The Digital Stock Market (DSM), a product of Wit Capital, evolved from a software program called the Chicago Match, which was tested for eight months on the Chicago Stock Exchange. It has SEC permission to bring after-hours trading and direct negotiating to online investors.

Sunlogic Securities Inc. (www.sunlogic.com) conducts after-hours trading via SelectNet for $40 an order, plus a $3 postage charge. Muriel Siebert & Co. Inc. (www.msiebert.com) executes trades after hours through the Instinet in addition to SelectNet.

Both Discover and Dreyfus brokerages offer extended trading for limit orders for 200 stocks—Monday through Thursday, from 6 to 8 pm Eastern time—through the extended hours marketplace, MarketXT, in development since 1997 in close participation with Bernard L. Madoff Investment Securities and Herzog Heine Geduld. In addition, investors may enter orders between the hours of 4:30 and 6:00 pm for execution when MarketXT opens at 6 pm. Market XT also features Volatility Alerts that advise whether a stock's price has changed more than 10% from close.

As demand increases, both the number of stocks and hours of operation will be expanded.

Technology is developing rapidly toward providing the individual investor a comfortable and convenient environment for trading on a level playing field with the pros. The more you understand the nuances and the differences between the brokerage sites, what types of trading they offer, and how they charge, the more control, consistency, and certainty you'll bring to your trading or investing. This book provides the basic comparative data that will help you take the first step to selecting the trading site to fit your needs.

GETTING CONNECTED

How to Choose Your Connection

For the investor who plans to buy and sell an occasional stock, a basic Internet service provider will be fine. For the more advanced user, dedicated connections wired to servers that add speed become more important. Now there are thousands of Internet services or access providers out there, ranging from national enterprises to small local businesses. These providers enable subscribers to connect to the Internet and use the Web. Because the competition is tough, the costs keep coming down for commercial online services such as America Online, CompuServe, Prodigy, and Microsoft Network.

For a list of Internet service providers (ISPs), visit www.thelist.com. It's called the ISP Buyer Guide. Here are some of the more popular national ISPs. (If you're reading this list, you probably aren't connected, so here are their 800 numbers):

AT&T World	1-800-967-5363
Internet MCI	1-800-955-5210
Netcom	1-800-353-6600
UUNET	1-800-488-6383

- If you first want to get your feet wet and make a few trades with a discount broker, the AOL Internet connection continues to improve and offers access to the Web. For more information call 1-800-827-6364 or visit the AOL Web site at www.aol.com.
- CompuServe has been established in the online world for a decade and offers the same basic monthly charges: 1-800-848-8990 or visit the CompuServe Web site at www.compuserve.com.
- Prodigy is family-oriented, geared toward general use. Contact 1-800-PRODIGY or the Prodigy Web site at www.prodigy.com.
- Microsoft Network System, MSN, is one of the newer online services. For more information, call 1-800-386-5550 or visit the Microsoft Web site at www.msn.com.

While some online brokerage firms provide access to the Web, others have special computer requirements and require proprietary software and startup fees. Still others are aimed toward the seasoned investor and not the novice. You may need more than your commercial online service. There are three tiers of Internet providers. Tier one—the digital subscriber line, DSL, connections—are the cleanest connections. The ISDN line connections, cable modems, and line ratios are a host of other considerations. Many sites have technical support to help you determine what will work best with their data feeds.

SEARCHING FOR SITES: For a shortcut to sites use Yahoo! You can find direct links to all the large retail brokerage sites, including most of the information links, as well as to Motley Fool and The Street.com. You can also construct stock and mutual fund portfolios.

SCREENING CAPABILITIES: Yahoo! Finance (www.yahoo.com) offers basic screening capabilities for free, based on eight data fields.

Intuit's Quicken.com (www.quicken.com) lets you sift through more than 10,600 stocks for free. Its screens include up to 33 variables. Say you want a stock with revenues of at least $1 billion, a five-year total return of at least 15%, a maximum price-earnings ratio of 16, and a current price within 5% of its 52-week high. You find 13 companies out of 10,000. Not too shabby.

If you want to concentrate on mutual funds, Go to Morningstar.net. You can track up to 10 portfolios with 50 securities in each for free. Use Morningstar's "Portfolio X-Rays" to determine whether holdings are over- or undervalued.

Opening an Account Online

Opening an account to trade electronically is basically the same as opening a traditional investment account at your brokerage office. You actually get access to the same tools that the professionals have without the need to obtain a Series 7 license. When you sign the papers to open an account, you must agree to all the traditional disclosure statements plus one—a disclosure form that means "warning" in legalese. Mostly, you are asked to attest in writing that you understand all the fees and regulations involved and you absolve the online broker of any unusual risks such as loss you might incur owing to an exchange computer system crash.

Online brokers are also required by the federal regulations to find out enough information from you to determine if you are suitable for the investment strategies that you plan to conduct. To do that, brokers must obtain the following information: your true name, actual street address (a post office box is not acceptable), principal occupation, current annual income, liquid net worth, total net worth, present age, citizenship, previous investment experience, investment objectives (whether short-term or electronic trades), marital status, number of dependents, and social security and tax identification numbers.

The rationale behind this inquiry is that the type of trading strategies you wish to employ are a critical part of your decision regarding the type of account you open. Margin accounts are governed by the Federal Reserve Board's Regulation T, which allows brokers to sell you stocks and finance 50 percent of the purchase. The Federal Reserve Board can adjust the figure up or down any time.

SITE SECURITY: Don't worry about hackers transferring assets out of your account—additional, offline security procedures prevent it. Most sites utilize 128-bit U.S. grade encryption and secure socket layer (SSL) protocol. In addition, like full service brokerage houses, the online trading sites carry SIPC (Securities Investor Protection Corporation) coverage, which will replace up to $500,000 in losses—including up to $100,000 cash—if the brokerage goes bankrupt.

If you have a problem or question, there are generally toll-free numbers to call or e-mail messaging. Some sites speed up the application process by offering forms for downloading, or forms you can print out directly from the site; others require a phone call or an e-mail request for forms.

Do You Have the Right Stuff?
Hardware and Communications

Very little serious trading software exists for Macs. In fact, most traders I've spoken with use two or more computers—one for hooking up to a chat room or news service, the other for their actual trades. Both computers should be 233 MHz or better and, ideally, hooked up to a fail-safe power source to protect against outages.

Having 128 MHz of memory will allow you to safely keep several windows open on the screen at once, which is something day trading software calls for, as you'll see. Likewise, because you'll want to be looking at several windows at once, it pays to invest in a large screen monitor.

Sam's Computers on the Net sells a $5755 system that makes use of four computer monitors, enough to track half a dozen different stocks and market indices at once. Windows NT 4.0 lets you run multiple monitors, and it's more fault-tolerant than its consumer cousin, Windows 98. Here, your choice might depend on the day trading broker you sign with. Some brokers offer direct dial-up connections via 56k modem or ISDN. This neatly avoids Internet bottlenecks, but you'll pay a hefty phone bill. An alternative is to invest in a cable modem or digital subscriber line (DSL), if these services exist where you live. Expect to pay $40 or more per month for either.

Many day traders recommend having two separate ISP accounts. That way, if one goes down, you have a backup. You'll also want at least two separate phone lines, with maybe a third to call your broker, shrink, or spiritual advisor during moments of extreme angst. Bottom line: Expect your communications bill to run $120 or more per month.

Specific site recommendations for hardware and accessories are included in many of the individual profiles. The standard Internet connection for trading includes:

CPU:	Pentium-based 133 (preferably 166) MHz processor.
Memory:	16 to 32 MB RAM.
Modem:	28.8k (preferably 56k).
Hard disk:	20 MB available space.
Operating system:	Windows 95/98 or NT 4.0 workstation.
Monitor:	14" color, 640 × 480 dpi resolution.
Software:	Latest Microsoft Explorer (some data software programs are MacIntosh and WebTV compatible).
Hookup:	Use a major ISP and connect via MCI, Sprint, IBM, or UUNET. Also DSL and ISI.

An upgrade for speed, efficiency, and access to some special site features might include:

CPU:	Pentium II 166 (preferably 200+) MHz.
Memory:	32 to 64 MB RAM.
Modem:	64/128k ISDN, 56v90 or 33.6v90k bps.
Hard disk:	2 to 4 GB.

Monitor:	17″ color, 800 × 600 dpi resolution (preferably multiple).
	If split monitors are used, Appian, STB, or Color Graphix installation is recommended.
Software:	Microsoft Excel spreadsheet, Adobe Acrobat Reader for downloading forms.

When you trade with an online discount broker, you may think that you are getting a good deal because your commissions are less than the other guy's. You may even have this feeling that you are trading directly with a market. But do you really know? It's time to find out. Here's what you should look for.

TIPS FOR SELECTING AN ONLINE BROKER

There's more to evaluate than who's offering the lowest commissions for online stock trades. Many online brokerage sites promote loss leaders by offering free or nearly free trades, but the bargain is for a type of trade you seldom make, or there's a shopping list of add-on fees.

Here are some points to consider when selecting an online broker.

1. **Compare apples with apples.** If you regularly make trades of 100 or 500 shares, check each broker's commission schedule for trades of those sizes. Occasionally, the lowest rate may apply only to trades of minimum level of assets in your account. Also, stocks priced under $1 a share will usually carry a higher commission. Look for less than $15 per trade for any number of shares. A rate below $21 is absolutely essential.

2. **Read the fine print.** Brokers charge for many things besides commissions. The Part II listings include any transaction or postage and handling fees that apply to all trades, but there are more fees that may be incurred. For example, it can cost as much as $25 to have a stock certificate issued and delivered into your hands. Rest assured that any service you request above and beyond the execution of a trade will cost you something. Make sure you know what that something is.

3. **Zero doesn't always equal zero.** Some brokers say they do not require a minimum initial investment. That doesn't mean they'll let you trade stocks without any money in your account! Before you make a purchase, any broker will require that some percentage—15%, 25%, or 50%—of the total cost of the trade be in your account. By the way, an IRA account will usually require a lower minimum investment than a regular account. And if you trade options, your broker will expect you to ante up a larger sum. These are spelled out somewhere on the site, usually when you click an Open an Account link.

4. **Low margin rates.** This rule applies to both small and large accounts. Most brokers offer margin accounts, which let you borrow against the equity in your account to buy more stocks. This is not a free service. You're charged an interest rate on the funds borrowed. Factor in the margin rate when you're at the decision-making point. For large customers, the rate should be lower than brokers call (currently 6½ percent). For small accounts, the rate should not be higher than 7¼ percent. Low margin rates are absolutely essential. Remember that, for all practical purposes, margin interest deductions will not affect your income taxes to any great extent. The IRS limits the amount of margin interest you can deduct in any one year.

5. **Buy into your specialty.** If you regularly trade options or bonds or mutual funds, make sure the broker you select trades those securities. Even if the broker trades them, they may not be traded over the Internet and may incur a higher than desirable commission. Be sure to check those commissions.

6. **You're on your own.** You need to be comfortable investing on your own: finding stock ideas, researching, making decisions, entering orders, and using a computer. Nobody holds your hand at the discount online firms; in fact, finding a human being to talk to at some firms can be like hunting for the invisible broker. If you're not comfortable with your own research and order entry on the computer, consider using a more full service broker like Merrill Lynch, Paine Webber, or Salomon Smith Barney. You'll pay more, but such firms can provide research reports, stock ideas, and market advice.

7. **Get rapid executions and confirmations of executed orders.** Confirming trades with discount online brokers can also be problematic. Depending on the broker you choose, you may get a phone call, e-mail, or even snail mail (U.S. Postal Service) to confirm a trade. If you need instant confirmation, make sure you get a broker who can provide it by telephone or e-mail. If you get yours in the mail two days after a trade and discover a problem, it could cost you a lot of money. If it's the broker's error and you can prove it, then the broker will make it right. If it's your error, you pay.

8. **Rapid account updates and availability of real-time quotes.** Look for instant updates after the completion of each order—as a bare minimum, an accurate account update by the beginning of each business day.

   More and more sites are adding real-time quotes, sometimes prorated based on the frequency of your trades. But real-time suffers some transmission or Internet-connection delays. Subscriber services for streaming quote data are available, but they usually carry a high premium and/or special software requirements. The type of trading you do will dictate the acceptability of the quote service.

9. **The ability to issue all types of orders online.** This ability should extend to short sales, AON (all-or-nothing) orders, and stop orders on both listed and OTC stocks. Ideally, bulletin board stocks, Pink Sheet listings, and a wide selection of foreign stocks are also available. Even if you've never issued an order to short, or any of the other orders, it is nice to have a broker who will accommodate the oddball request on those few occasions when you want it.

10. **Onsite charts, news, and research information.** Much information is available on other Web sites, but it's a nice feature for brokers to offer as well.

11. **Availability of options at reasonable rates and no-fee IRA accounts.** Reasonable means below $20 for one option, below $30 for five options, and below $40 for ten options.

12. **Availability of other services and perks.** These include mutual funds, free checking, credit cards, debit cards, Web TV compatibility, research, 24-hour service, tools options, and minimum balances. Some brokers offer rewards for frequent traders in the form of reduced commissions and even frequent flyer miles.

13. **Good customer service.** Service is essential in the event that problems arise when trading online. Look for ready availability of courteous live brokers. If you are looking for a new broker, telephone several prospective brokers a few times, asking questions about services of interest. Then avoid those brokers whom you can't reach after a few rings. Is there an 800 number that you can call for help? How responsive is the broker to an e-mail? Look at emergency back-up measures: touch-tone orders or personal broker availability? It all comes down to customer support.

CHOOSING THE RIGHT ORDER

Finally, here is a description of the kinds of orders you can place and how they affect an execution.

MARKET ORDER: A market order will typically assure you an execution, but not a specific price. When you send a market order, you ask for it to be filled at whatever price is available when your order reaches its destination. In a volatile market, the fill price can be substantially different from the price that was quoted.

LIMIT ORDER: A limit order is an order to buy or sell a stock with a price restriction. A buy limit sets the maximum price you are willing to pay, and a sell limit sets the minimum price at which you are willing to sell. It guarantees you a specific price, but it does not guarantee you an execution.

For example, you may wish to purchase a stock that is currently quoted at 15 bid, 15¼ ask, but you do not want to pay more than $14. If you place a limit order at $14, it will be filled only if the price drops to $14 or lower and there are no orders ahead of yours. If the stock continues to trade at its current quote, you will not receive an execution.

STOP ORDER: A stop order is an order designed to protect a profit or guard against a loss. Although it does not work well in all conditions, it can be an effective strategy in certain situations. When placing a stop order, you specify a stop price that, when reached, converts your order to a market order.

For example, you may have purchased XZY stock at $40 and it is now trading at $60. If XZY drops to $50, you want to sell the stock. You can place a sell stop order at $50, and if the stock trades there, your order becomes a market order to sell. The risk with this type of order is that once triggered, your order can be filled at any price because it is a market order.

STOP LIMIT ORDER: A stop limit order is a variation on the stop order. It works in a similar fashion in that it is triggered once the stock hits the stop price, but instead of becoming a market order, it becomes a limit order at a price that you select. Limit orders in a fast market will reduce your risk of receiving an unexpected execution price. What's more, a limit order allows you to place an order at the price level you're most comfortable with when buying or selling a security. Although a limit order does not guarantee that your order will be executed, it does guarantee that you will not pay a higher price than you expected.

For example, you want to limit losses on a stock that you purchased at $50. You enter a sell stop limit order at "$40 Stop $39 Limit." Once the stock trades at $40 or below, your order becomes a limit order to sell at $39. This will ensure that you do not sell at an extremely low price if a stock opens drastically lower. However, you will still own the stock, since the order was not executed.

Each of the above orders has its pros and cons. You should pick the order that is best for your situation and considers current market conditions.

USEFUL ABBREVIATIONS

There are many abbreviations that appear throughout the book, especially in the Part 2 profiles. The following key will guide you in understanding any abbreviations that may not be fully explained where they occur.

ADR   American depositary receipt
AON   all or nothing
BB   bulletin board
DOT   direct order turnaround
ECN   electronic communications network
FAQ   frequently asked question
GTC   good till canceled
IPO   initial public offering
IRA   individual retirement account
PDA   personal digital assistant
SOES   small order execution system

In addition to the "generic" abbreviations above, following are some ECN "finders" that seek the best method of order execution, whether it is a market maker or an ECN.

ARCA   Archipelago
ATTN   Attain
BTRD   Bloomberg
INCA   Instinet
ISLD   Island
REDI   Speer, Leeds & Kellogg
TNTO   Terra Nova

Depending on which ECN is "hit," there is an extra fee per share that is listed in the fee area of this site. Orders are executed within seconds! ECNs work as order matching systems and allow traders to advertise a price better than the current bid or offer.

Part 2

Online Trading Sites

Discount Online Trading Sites

The following sites vary widely, from full service brokerage firms offering discounted online trading to deep discount online brokerages, but they mostly meet the needs of the investor who holds positions from intermediate to long-term.

The site descriptions are intentionally positioned to provide blank space for *your* notes, updates, and rating.

ACCUTRADE, INC.

URL: www.accutrade.com

TYPE OF SITE: Discount brokerage

USERS: Online traders needing little assistance

SNAIL MAIL: 4211 S. 102nd Street
Omaha, NE 68103-2227

PHONE: 1-800-882-4887

E-MAIL: info@accutrade.com

SERVICES: Access Accutrade trading system via Internet, Accutrade for Windows®, fax at 1-800-821-0743 with online fax trading form, touch-tone phone 1-800-222-2228, PC secure dial-up system, and Sharp® Zaurus™ personal digital assistant (PDA), or live broker. Download account reports to Quicken 98 (1-800-555-4137) and Money 98 (1-800-882-4887). Customizable portfolio tracker and quote list; asset allocation worksheet; stock and fund alerts.

EXECUTION SYSTEMS: Accutrade's order desk.

FEES:

Account minimum: $5000 initial deposit; $2000 for IRA account.

Quotes: Delayed quotes + 100 free real-time quotes per Internet-executed trade. $20 for unlimited real-time quotes. PC or touch-tone phone receives 15 minutes of complimentary quote time upon activation plus 30 minutes at first sign-off from PC; plus 4 minutes for each executed trade. Call 1-800-229-3011 for necessary forms to receive real-time quotes via PC.

Trades: $29.95/trade up to 1000 shares, plus $.02/additional share over 1000. 3 free trades with account activation.

Mutual funds: Flat fee of $27/transaction if required; no-load funds have no fees if held for at least 6 months. Access to over 6000 funds.

Bonds: Agency bond trades—$5/bond up to 50 bonds, and $2.50/bond over 50. $40 minimum commission.

Options: $35 minimum commission; graduated fee per contract based on premium and quantity.

APPEALING FEATURES: Asset allocation worksheet.

SUPPORT SYSTEMS: 1-800-555-4137 during normal business hours or e-mail accuhelp@accutrade.com. Free informational booklets available at 1-800-228-3011; standard glossary. Research includes one free S&P stock report per executed trade from 1-800-228-3011, plus Ford Research Data, Company Screening, Fund Screening, Market Monitor, Mutual Fund Monitor, Municipal Bond Guide. Direct connection to Insider Trading Watch, Dow Jones News, Morningstar.net, ISS Friday Report, EDGAR Online, Big Charts, and Motley Fool; plus subscription to Market Edge investment tools and stock analysis.

Open account with forms downloaded from site.

OPERATIONAL SYSTEMS:
CPU: Pentium-based with minimum 200 MHz processor.
Memory: 64MB RAM.
Hard disk: 20 MB minimum (2GB or even 4GB recommended).
Modem: 56k analog Internet connection, and ISDN; cable modem, DSL, and ADSL acceptable.
Operating system: Win95/98 with 2MB video card.

BACKGROUND INFORMATION: Accutrade, member NASD/SIPC, began offering discount brokerage services in 1975.

AMERICA FIRST ASSOCIATES—AF TRADER

URL: www.aftrader.com

TYPE OF SITE: Full-service broker offering online, touch-tone, and advisor trading.

USERS: All levels of online investors.

SNAIL MAIL: 415 Madison Avenue, 3d Floor
New York, NY 10017

PHONE: 1-888-OTC-NYSE (682-6973)

E-MAIL: support@aftrader.com

SERVICES: Integrated banking and investing services.

EXECUTION SYSTEMS: Clearing company is U.S. Clearing, a division of Fleet Securities, Inc.

FEES:

Account minimum: None.

Quotes: Free unlimited real-time quotes.

Limit/market trades: Listed and OTC—$14.95/trade, up to 5000 shares. Over 5000 shares, add $.01/share for entire order (e.g., $114.95 for 10,000 shares).

Touch-tone: 1-800-362-6275. Extra $5/trade.

Broker-assisted: $30/trade.

BB and penny stocks: $14.95/trade, up to 5000 shares (and/or up to $10,000 stock value), then add $.01/share for entire order.

Mutual funds: $30/trade for no-loads; 2500+ funds to choose from.

IRA accounts: Free; free setup; closing $50.

Options: $25 + $1.75/contract (Internet or touch-tone). Add $25 for broker assistance.

Bonds: Corporate and zero coupon—lesser of $10 per $1000 face amount or 1% of principal; $50 minimum.

Treasuries: $50/trade for bills, notes, or bonds.

Margin: $7\frac{1}{4}$% to $8\frac{1}{2}$%; brokers call plus $\frac{3}{4}$% to 2%.

APPEALING FEATURES: Free research/news, including Zacks, 2nd Opinion, Briefing.com.

SUPPORT SYSTEMS: Toll-free number with voice mail. Glossary and demo.

Open account online; one business day approval.

OPERATIONAL SYSTEMS:

CPU: Pentium-based with minimum 166 MHz processor (200+ recommended).

Memory: 32MB RAM (64MB recommended).

Hard disk: 20 MB minimum (2GB or even 4GB recommended).

Modem: 64/128k ISDN, 56v90 or 33.6v90 kbps.

Operating system: Win95/98 or NT 4.0 with SP3 applied.

Browser: Microsoft Explorer.

BACKGROUND INFORMATION: America First Associates is a member of NASD/SIPC and MSRB.

AMERITRADE HOLDING CORP.

URL: www.ameritrade.com

TYPE OF SITE: Deep discount broker, with advanced options for trading online.

USERS: Online traders.

SNAIL MAIL: Ameritrade Holding Corp.
140 Broadway, 46th floor
New York, NY 10005-1101

PHONE: 1-800-454-9272

E-MAIL: starting@ameritrade.com

SERVICES: Allows traders complete control of their investments online, including option and equity orders, with 35-symbol hot quote list, positions, account balances, and transaction history. Provides basic, intermediate, or advanced order tickets, including advanced option order ticket to place spread, straddle, and strangle orders online.

EXECUTION SYSTEMS: Clearing firm is Advanced Clearing, established in 1985.

FEES:

Account minimum: $2000. Interest paid on balance over $1000. $800 annual commission includes maximum 240 trades on accounts $10,000+, 200+ shares per order.

Quotes: $20/month for unlimited real-time quotes. Otherwise, 100 free real-time quotes on sign-up; additional 100 free per trade. PDA Zaurus—$20/month, plus $.25/minute; 2 minutes free for each executed trade. Touch-tone—$.25/minute; 2 minutes free quote time for each executed trade.

Trades: Market—$8 for any number of shares. Limit/stop—add $5/trade for any number of shares.

Touch-tone: 1-800-669-3900. Add $4/trade.

Broker-assisted: Add $10/trade.

Options: $25 + $1.75 per contract; 10% discount on trades placed electronically. Internet and touch-tone—$29 minimum commission. Option exercises and assignments incur an $18 commission.

BB and penny stocks: $18–$23/trade for 20,000 shares @ $.50. BB must be ordered through live assistant.

Canadian stocks: $.02/share (+ $23 limit—$53 minimum); or (+ $18 market—$48 minimum). $173 maximum.

Mutual funds: $18/trade (1600+ funds to choose from).

IRA accounts: Free; free setup; closing $25.

Margin: 6% to 8½%: prime rate plus .75% to less 1.75%.

APPEALING FEATURES: *Darwin: Survival of the Fittest,* free simulated options trading CD game.

SUPPORT SYSTEMS: Toll-free number open 24 hours from 9 pm Sun to 9 pm Fri, CST. Glossary, integrated page help, log-in from any page. Screen shot demo of Internet and touch-tone trading. Research/news includes Quick Facts, Stock Quest, Market Guide, PR Newswire, Businesswire, Dow Jones News.

OPERATIONAL SYSTEMS:

CPU: Pentium-based with minimum 166 MHz processor (200+ recommended).

Memory: 32MB RAM (64MB recommended).

Hard disk: minimum 20 MB (2GB or even 4GB recommended).

Modem: 64/128k ISDN, 56v90 or 33.6v90 kbps.

Operating system: Win95/98 or NT 4.0 with SP3 applied.

Browser: Microsoft Explorer.

BACKGROUND INFORMATION: Ameritrade Holding Corp. launched Ameritrade in 1997, combining the most popular features of its prior acquisition, K. Aufhauser & Co. (the first to offer Internet trading in 1994), with Ceres Securities and eBroker™ (AHC's Internet-only brokerage). Ameritrade offered breakthrough pricing at "8 Bucks" for Internet trades and was the first brokerage to offer advanced option tickets (spreads, straddles, and buy/writes) on the Internet. Ameritrade also introduced electronic trade confirmations by e-mail.

ANDREW PECK ASSOCIATES, INC.

URL: www.andrewpeck.com

TYPE OF SITE: Full service brokerage firm offering online trading.

USERS: Online traders needing little or no assistance.

SNAIL MAIL: Newport Financial Center
111 Pavonia Avenue
Jersey City, NJ 07310

PHONE: 1-800-221-5873

E-MAIL: andrewpeck@smartserv.com

SERVICES: Account information and stock quotes on any listed or Nasdaq securities and options.

EXECUTION SYSTEMS: Clearing firm is Schroder & Co., Inc.

FEES:

Account minimum: None.

Quotes: Real-time quotes and tick-by-tick updates via PC and the Web.

Limit/market trades: Limited-time offer—$.01/share (minimum $24/trade). Savings in size (3000 shares per trade regularly, any price stock)—$.03/share on listed stocks ($100 minimum per trade); $.02/share on OTC stocks ($75 minimum per trade). Retail (regularly trade less than 3000 shares per trade, any price stock)—$40 base charge plus: $.08/share for up to 499 shares, or $.06½/share for 500–999 shares, or $.05/share for 1000–2499 shares, or $.04/share over 2500 shares (minimum $50/trade).

Options: $1.90 for ¹⁄₁₆–⁷⁄₁₆; $2.20 for ½–¹⁵⁄₁₆; $2.40 for 1–1¹⁵⁄₁₆; $3 for 2–3⁷⁄₈; $4 for 4–7⁷⁄₈; $6 for 8 and over.

Bonds: Corporate and municipal—$5/bond ($50 minimum).

Margin: Related to brokers call money rate as published in financial newspapers.

APPEALING FEATURES: Free unlimited real-time quotes.

SUPPORT SYSTEMS: Toll-free number during market hours.

OPERATIONAL SYSTEMS: Standard.

BACKGROUND INFORMATION: Andrew Peck Associates, Inc., member NASD/SIPC, was founded in 1979.

BANK OF MONTREAL INVESTORLINE

URL: www.investorline.com

TYPE OF SITE: Full service Canadian brokerage offering online, touch-tone, or broker-assisted trading of Nasdaq and Canadian OTC— aka Canadian Dealing Network (CDN).

USERS: Canadian and U.S. online investors.

SNAIL MAIL: 2015 Peel Street, 2nd Floor
Montreal, Quebec H3A ITB

PHONE: 1-800-387-7800

SERVICES: Automated telephone trading (1-888-776-6886). U.S. data supplied by North American Quotation. Canadian data supplied by Canadian Stock Market Reporter. Gold pricing by Kito.com. Dynamic portfolio management report.

FEES:

Account minimum: None. Deposit must be received in new account to execute first trade. No fees for nonregistered account.

Quotes: Free real-time quotes when signed to online account; otherwise, 15-minute delay.

Trades (online or touch-tone): Market—$25 up to 1000 shares, any value. Limit—$29 up to 1000 shares, any value. Both market and limit—Over 1000 shares, add $.005/share for stock value $0–$1, $.02/share for stock value $1.01–$5; and $.03/share for stock value over $5.

Broker-assisted: Maximum commission is 2½% of principal value of trade, subject to a minimum of $35. When value of trade is $2000 or less, maximum commission is $35. For trades over $2000: Nasdaq—add $.02/share for stock value up to $1 and an additional $.01/share at stock value price breaks of $2, $5, $10, $20, $30, and over (e.g., commission on 150 shares @ $21 is $45.50). CDN— add $.005/share for stock value up to $1, $.02/share for stock value of $1.01–$5, and $.01/share at stock value price breaks of $10, $20, $30, and over (e.g., commission on 150 shares @ $21 is $42.50).

Mutual funds: 2% of value up to $25,000; 1% over $25,000. Minimum $25/trade for front-end purchase. No fee for no-load purchase, $40 for no-load redemption, no fee for redemption of 1st Canadian. Online or automated telephone trading orders receive 20% discount off regular charges. 750+ mutual funds offered.

Options: Minimum of $29/trade. Add $1/contract if option price is $1 or less, $1.50 if option price is $1.01–$2, $2 if option price is $2.01–$3, $2.50 if option price is $3.01–$4, $3 if option price is $4.01–$5, and $3.50 if option price is over $5. Online or automated telephone trading orders receive 20% discount off regular charges.

Bonds, strips, T-bills, GICs: Through broker only. Commissions, if any, are included in quoted price.

Margin: Line of credit in Canadian or U.S. dollars at Bank of Montreal prime + 1% per annum.

APPEALING FEATURES: Canadian securities.

SUPPORT SYSTEMS: Toll-free number available 24 hours daily. Demo with interactive screen. Research/news includes free Carlson Online; specialized subscription services such as market research tools available at discount. News, charts, and more available 24 hours daily. Historical and current end-of-day data provided by Interactive Data Corp. NewsLine™ quarterly newsletter. FundFinder® mutual fund research tool. Borrowing and retirement planning calculators.

OPERATIONAL SYSTEMS: Standard.

BACKGROUND INFORMATION: Bank of Montreal Investorline is the electronic brokerage division of Bank of Montreal.

BENSON YORK GROUP, INC.—MOSTACTIVES

URL: www.mostactives.com

TYPE OF SITE: Full service brokerage with remote trading capabilities.

USERS: Online traders of all levels. Check site "Open an Account" page for availability in your state.

SNAIL MAIL: 8723 Fourth Avenue
Brooklyn, NY 11200

PHONE: 1-888-409-4773

E-MAIL: customerservice@mostactives.com
webmaster@mostactives.com

SERVICES: Trading access through Internet, touch-tone phone, wireless, and full service brokers. Options and bonds permitted.

EXECUTION SYSTEMS: Executes trades during market hours. Clears all transactions through J. B. Oxford & Company.

FEES:
Account minimum: None.
Quotes: Link to data feed, DTN.IQ, subscription (one week free trial with online sign-up)—$79/month plus exchange fees, plus $50 initiation fee. Includes unlimited streaming real-time quotes, trading and portfolio management program.
Trades: $9.99/trade, +$3/trade for postage/handling; add $.02/share for listed stocks; add $5/trade for limit orders. $10/trade extra for broker assistance. No extra charge for touch-tone orders. Add ECN fees when applicable (currently $.015/share/trade).
Options: $25 + $2.50/contract.
Bonds: $5/bond ($50 minimum).

APPEALING FEATURES: Online investor training course in modules, plus fully loaded computer store.

SUPPORT SYSTEMS: Toll-free order entry assistance (add $10/trade); technical support available by phone or e-mail. Free research.
Open account by e-mailing online application request.

OPERATIONAL SYSTEMS:

CPU: Pentium-based with minimum 166 MHz processor (200+ recommended).

Memory: 32MB RAM (64MB recommended).

Hard disk: 20 MB minimum (2GB or even 4GB recommended).

Modem: 64/128k ISDN, 56v90 or 33.6v90 kbps.

Operating system: Win95/98 or NT 4.0 with SP3 applied.

Browser: Microsoft Explorer.

BACKGROUND INFORMATION: Benson York Group Inc., member NASD/SIPC, was founded in 1995 by President Michael Caldera, and introduced its remote trading facility, MostActives.com (recently renamed from BuyStocks.com), utilizing automated trade confirmations by telephone with a computerized human voice.

BIDWELL & COMPANY

URL: www.bidwell.com

TYPE OF SITE: Full service discount broker, all major securities markets.

USERS: Online investors, individuals and institutional; foreign accounts accepted.

SNAIL MAIL: 209 SW Oak Street
               Portland, OR 97204-2791

PHONE: 1-800-547-6337

E-MAIL: info@bidwell.com

SERVICES: State-of-the-art information technology provides real-time capability for order executions.

EXECUTION SYSTEMS: Self-clearing (no third party). Verbal or e-mail confirmation in addition to mailed written confirmation.

FEES:

Account minimum: None. All orders subject to $1.25 postage/handling fee. Free dividend reinvestment.

Quotes: 100 free real-time quotes on opening account; additional 100 quotes per trade.

Trades: Limit (Web and touch-tone)—$15 up to 1500 shares; over 1500 shares, $.01/share for entire order; plus $1.25 postage/handling fee (e.g., $51.25 for 5000 shares). Market (Web and touch-tone)—$12 up to 1500 shares; over 1500 shares, $.01/share for entire order; plus $1.25 postage/handling fee (e.g., $101.25 for 10,000 shares).

Touch-Tone Trade™: 1-800-215-9262. Create quote lists to track portfolio and trade 24 hours daily. Access code is last 4 digits of Social Security number used to open account.

Broker-assisted: $20 + $1.25 postage/handling fee per trade, plus $.05–$.08/share for first 500 shares (based on value breaks at over $10, $20, $30), plus $.03/share over 500. 5% of principal for OTC securities under $1/share, subject to a $20 minimum.

Penny stocks: 5% of principal; $21.25 minimum (e.g., $500 for 20,000 shares @ $.50).

Mutual funds: $25/trade + $.0015 of principal + $1.25 postage/handling fee for no-loads. For front-end, the load fee charged is subject to a minimum of the above. No transaction fee to Bidwell FundSource mutual funds.

IRA accounts: $25/year.

Options: $27 + $3/contract + $1.25 postage/handling fee.

Bonds: Municipal and corporate—$5/bond with $50 minimum. Zero coupon—lesser of 1% of principal or $4/bond with $30 minimum.

Treasuries: Bills, $25/trade. Notes, $3/note with $30 minimum. Bonds. $5/bond with $50 minimum.

APPEALING FEATURES: Commission calculator.

SUPPORT SYSTEMS: Toll-free number available 6 am–5 pm PST; after hours, 1-503-790-9000 ext. 1. Standard glossary, online seminar schedule, quarterly newsletter with monthly account statement. Dynamic portfolio management report, commission calculator. Interactive demo screen.

OPERATIONAL SYSTEMS: Standard.

BACKGROUND INFORMATION: Bidwell & Company, member SIPC, NASD, was founded in 1985.

BROWN & CO.

URL: www.brownco.com

TYPE OF SITE: Deep discount broker. No mutual funds. Trade via broker, online, DirectLine, touch-tone, or PC Line systems.

USERS: Substantial traders with experience; U.S. residents only.

SNAIL MAIL: One Beacon Street
             Boston, MA 02108

PHONE: 1-800-225-6707

SERVICES: Beta-testing next phase of Web site. Has 150 registered reps, plus offices throughout the U.S., to assist trading.

EXECUTION SYSTEMS: Brown & Co.'s order desk sells order flow.

FEES:

Account minimum: $15,000; annual income of at least $40,000, net worth (exclusive of real estate) of $50,000, and 5 years of market experience. No minimum account activity. 10% rebate on commissions exceeding $350/month. Interest paid on credit balances over $1000.

Quotes: Free real-time stock and option quotes online; 100 free real-time quotes per trade.

Trades: Limit (online and touch-tone)—$10 up to 5000 shares; over 5000 shares, add $.01/share for entire order (e.g., $110 for 10,000 shares). No stop/limit orders online.

Market (online and touch-tone)—$5 up to 5000 shares; over 5000 shares, add $.01/share for entire order (e.g., $105 for 10,000 shares).

Broker-assisted: $12 market and $17 for limit trades for up to 5000 shares, then add $.01/share for entire order. $20 + $1.75/contract for options ($25 minimum).

Rebate: 10% of total commission during months that commissions exceed $350.

IRA accounts: Free.

Options: $25 minimum online. $15 + $1.75/contract for limit orders. Assignments $19. $15 + $1.50/contract for up to 30 contracts, then $1.75/contract. Spreads accepted.

Bonds: Listed—$4/bond; minimum commission $30 per order.
Treasuries: $50/transaction.
Margin: 5½% to 6½%: brokers call to 1%.

SUPPORT SYSTEMS: 1-800-822-2021 Mon–Fri, plus voice mail. Links to free research. Portfolio management report, trades confirmed by phone or fax—and mail; monthly statement by mail.

OPERATIONAL SYSTEMS: Standard.

BACKGROUND INFORMATION: Brown & Co., member NASD/SIPC, was established in 1960 and is a subsidiary of Chase Manhattan Bank.

BULL & BEAR SECURITIES, INC.

URL: www.bullbear.com

TYPE OF SITE: Discount brokerage.

USERS: Online traders.

SNAIL MAIL: 11 Hanover Square
New York, NY 10005

PHONE: 1-800-BULLBEAR (285-5232)

E-MAIL: info@bullbear.com

SERVICES: Delayed quotes, option quotes/chains, price history, intraday graphs, Java charts, currency rates, equity indices, IPO info, INC link, Standard & Poor's. Dynamic portfolio management report, order verification page, confirmation reference number.

EXECUTION SYSTEMS: Clearing company is U.S. Clearing, a division of Fleet Securities, Inc.

FEES:

Account minimum: None. Free dividend reinvestment, checking, and debit card.

Limit/market trades: $19.95 up to 1000 shares; above 1000, add $.02/share (e.g., $99.95 for 5000 shares). Foreign stock valued at less than $3/share—2% of principal. U.S. stock valued at less than $1/share—$31 + 3.2% of principal.

Touch-tone quote retrieval and trading: 20% discount off regular commission schedule.

Broker-assisted: Based on transaction values minimum: $.072/share up to 1000 shares, plus $.032/share over 1000 shares for stocks valued below $5/share $.04/share over 1000 shares for stocks valued at $5 or greater/share.

Maximum: $44 for first 100 shares, plus $.44/share thereafter.

Options: $39/trade minimum. Selling at $.50 or under—sliding scale based on number of contracts. Selling at greater than $.50—sliding scale based on transaction size.

Mutual funds: $23/trade minimum, sliding scale based on transaction size.

Bonds: Municipal and corporate—$31/trade minimum: $4/bond on first 25 bonds and $2.40/bond or, if less, .8% of principal.

IRA accounts: Free, no setup fee, $50 to close.

Treasuries: $31/trade.

Margin: 8% on $25,000.

APPEALING FEATURES: Trading earns miles on American Airlines.

SUPPORT SYSTEMS: 1-800-BNB-5800 (262-5800); broker available 8:30 am–5 pm EST; 24-hour news and info. Standard glossary, demo, online symbol lookup, hot stock list, contextual help feature.

OPERATIONAL SYSTEMS: Standard.

BACKGROUND INFORMATION: Bull & Bear Securities, Inc., member NASD/SIPC, was recently acquired by Royal Bank of Canada Financial Group.

BURKE, CHRISTENSEN & LEWIS SECURITIES, INC.—BCL ONLINE

URL: www.bclnet.com

TYPE OF SITE: Discount brokerage offering online, touch-tone, and broker rep trading. Web TV compatible.

USERS: Online traders, U.S. residents only.

SNAIL MAIL: 303 W. Madison Street, Suite 400
Chicago, IL 60606

PHONE: 1-800-621-0392

SERVICES: Trading Access allows traders to enter order online. Balance and Position Access provides online account information.

EXECUTION SYSTEMS: A self-clearing firm, BCL is a member of the Depository Trust Company (DTC), the National Securities Clearing Corporation (NSCC), and the Options Clearing Corporation (OCC).

FEES:

Account minimum: None. No minimum number of trades.

Quotes: Free unlimited delayed stock and option quotes. 100 free real-time quotes on opening account; additional 100 per trade.

Trades: Limit—*NetRep*, $18/trade up to 5000 shares; over 5000 shares, $.01/share for entire order (e.g., $100 for 10,000 shares). Market—*NetRep*, $13/trade up to 5000 shares; over 5000 shares, $.01/share for entire order (e.g., $100 for 10,000 shares).

Touch-tone: TeleRep, 20% discount off broker-assisted rates; $34 minimum/trade.

Broker-assisted: Value-based with $34 minimum; 100 shares for $34; $53–$175 for 1000 shares; $200–$265 for 5000 shares.

Penny stocks: $30 + $7 per 1000 shares ($34 minimum); $170 for 20,000 shares @ $.50 share.

IRA accounts: Free.

Options: Nononline—$27 + $1.50/contract + .0035 of principal. Online—10% off regular cost. No uncovered options writing online.

Margin: $7\frac{1}{2}$%: brokers call plus 1%. Free dividend reinvestment.

SUPPORT SYSTEMS: Customer service at 1-800-621-0392, plus area-specific contact list. Research includes TheStreet.com, Financial Information Center, Mutual Fund Center, charts, and more.

Online request form to open account.

OPERATIONAL SYSTEMS:

Software: A security-enabled Internet browser, such as Netscape Navigator (recommended) 3.0 or greater, or Microsoft Internet Explorer 3.0 or greater, and Windows 95. The Netscape browser can be downloaded free from Netscape.

Hardware: At least a 486 66MHz PC with 16MB RAM (Pentium-based with 16MB+ recommended) and a 28.8k modem (33.6k + recommended).

BACKGROUND INFORMATION: Burke, Christensen & Lewis Securities, member NASD/SIPC and MSRB, was one of the first discount brokers in the country when it opened in 1973.

CALES INVESTMENTS, INC.

URL: www.calesinvestments.com

TYPE OF SITE: Full service brokerage firm with offices in Colorado and Germany. Also foreign securities.

USERS: Online investors. Currently available for Colorado, Texas, and Wyoming residents.

SNAIL MAIL: 925 Clarkson Street
Denver, CO 80218

PHONE: 1-303-863-8272

E-MAIL: hvohs@calesinvestments.com

SERVICES: Quote.com Inc. delivers NYSE, Nasdaq, and AMEX delayed 15–20 minutes. Account holders get snapshot quotes. Research through Zacks, Lipper, Groups Foreign Exchange, intraday charts, indices. Global asset management and introduction to foreign investment banks for international investments.

EXECUTION SYSTEMS: Clearing company is Southwest Securities.

FEES:
Account minimum: $2500 initial.
Limit/market trades: $19.95 up to 5000 shares; $.01/share thereafter.
Broker-assisted: Call or e-mail for specific transaction cost.
Mutual funds: Through broker; call or e-mail for costs.
Options: Per contract quantity; volume discounts.
Margin: Borrow a maximum of 50% of current value of marginable securities held in account.

APPEALING FEATURES: In-depth informational section on how to choose investments—government bonds, corporate bonds, zero coupon bonds, GNMA, money market funds, mutual funds, common stock, preferred stock, utility stocks, limited partnerships, options, covered options, insider trading.

SUPPORT SYSTEMS: Live assistance Mon–Fri, 7:30 am–5 pm CST. Plus voice mail and 24-hour e-mail. Symbol search.

OPERATIONAL SYSTEMS: Standard.

BACKGROUND FEATURES: Cales Investments Inc. is a member of NASD/SIPC.

CAPITAL INTERNATIONAL
SECURITIES GROUP, INC.—NET-INVEST

URL: www.net-invest.com

TYPE OF SITE: Full service broker with online and investment banking, including IPOs online.

USERS: Substantial online traders.

SNAIL MAIL: 1 SE Third Avenue, 22nd Floor
           Miami, FL 33131

PHONE: 1-800-584-7796

E-MAIL: memberservices@net-invest.com

SERVICES: Full range of Internet-based services, stock quotes, online research, online stock and mutual fund order entry, and full account access, all secured by SSL encryption. Pershing research free to accounts with $40,000 net equity; otherwise, $25/month.

EXECUTION SYSTEMS: Trades executed during market hours only. Clearing agent is Pershing, a division of Donaldson, Lufkin & Jenrette Securities Corporation.

FEES:
>*Account minimum:* $10,000 to activate; if equity falls below $2000, account will be closed. $25 annual maintenance fee waived for accounts with $40,000 net equity.
>*Quotes:* Unlimited real-time quotes free to accounts with $40,000 net equity; otherwise, $20/month.
>*Trades:* OTC buy/sell—$24.95. Listed buy/sell—$24.95 + $.02/share if over 2000 shares.
>*Mutual funds:* Purchase/redemption, $24.95.
>*Options:* Buy/sell, $24.95 + $1.50/contract.
>*Bonds:* Buy/sell, $35.

APPEALING FEATURES: IPO offerings.

SUPPORT SYSTEMS: Broker assistance with trades, 1-305-925-1060. Support, 1-800-967-9801 and techsupport@net-invet.com. Trading demo, newsletter. Account reports include portfolio management page, real-time order status; full trade blotter allows for open order changes/cancellations.

OPERATIONAL SYSTEMS: Standard.

BACKGROUND INFORMATION: Net-invest.com is a service of Capital International Security Group, Inc. Capital International is a full service brokerage firm founded in January 1992. Headquartered in Miami, FL, it also has branch offices in Tampa and Naples, and in New York City.

CITICORP INVESTMENT SERVICES

URL: www.citibank.com/us/investments

TYPE OF SITE: Full service brokerage with integrated banking services; trading accessed by broker, online, touch-tone, and ATM.

USERS: Online investors, Citibank account holders. No foreign accounts.

SNAIL MAIL: 111 Wall Street, 3rd Floor
New York, NY 10043

PHONE: 1-800-ASK-CITI (275-2484) ext. 0263

SERVICES: Delayed quotes. Up to 7 portfolio trackers and custom quote lists; commission calculator. Free personal investment plan assistance. Profiles, charts, news, Market Guide's quick facts, Zacks II earnings estimates, and Telescon ProSearch criteria report.

FEES:

Account minimum: $50 annual maintenance fee assessed when no transactions occur for 12 months in account with average monthly balances less than $10,000.

Limit/market trades: DirectAccess® provides $19.95 per online trade up to 10,000 shares (maximum value $100,000). Add $2.50 postage/handling fee per trade. $3 fee for dividend reinvestment per equity per dividend period.

Touch-tone: Fees same as online. CitiPhone Trading®, 24 hours daily, provides real-time quotes, portfolio and trading (1-800-846-5200, option 1, outside NY).

ATM: Fees same as online. Trading through Citibank ATMs.

Broker-assisted: $29.95/trade for up to 100 shares; $20 + $.18/share for 101–500 shares; $85 + $.04/share for 501–1000 shares; $100 + $.02/share for 1000+ shares. Stocks under $1—the greater of $29.95 or 3% of principal. Plus $5 postage/handling fee per trade by broker or phone (1-800-846-5200, option 3, outside NY).

Mutual funds: Over 4000 to choose from, plus CitiFunds™ and Citi-Select®.

Bonds: Agency bond trades are $5/bond up to 20 bonds, and $2/bond over 20 bonds. $29.95 minimum commission. Electronic trades receive 20% commission discount.

Treasuries: Agency trades are $50.

APPEALING FEATURES: ATM securities trading.

SUPPORT SYSTEMS: Toll-free number, e-mail, standard glossary, planning tools, FAQs.

OPERATIONAL SYSTEMS: Standard.

BACKGROUND INFORMATION: Citicorp Investment Services, member NASD/SIPC, is an affiliate of Citibank.

COMPUTEL SECURITIES

URL: www.computel.com

TYPE OF SITE: Full service brokerage.

USERS: Online investors using Internet or touch-tone phone.

SNAIL MAIL: 301 Mission Street, 5th Floor
San Francisco, CA 94105

PHONE: 1-800-432-0327

E-MAIL: support@computel.com

SERVICES: Portfolio management report with order status, execution summary, and positions page; verbal or automated confirmations—written confirmation mailed next business day; monthly statement.

EXECUTION SYSTEMS: Clearing company is U.S. Clearing Corp.

FEES:

Account minimum: None noted. No annual fees. No connect-time fees to CompuTel via Internet or touch-tone (1-888-240-2835).

Quotes: 24 free real-time quotes per day; unlimited delayed.

Data fees: Subscription available to Signal Online™ at $59/month and StockEdge Online™ at $130/month. Free to Premier accounts (equity balance of $250,000).

Trades: Limit—$19 + $2.50 postage/handling fee per trade. Market—$9 for trades of 1000–5000 shares; $14 for trades less than 1000 shares; plus $2.50 postage/handling fee per trade. $19.95 + 2% of principal per trade for stocks priced under $2 and Canadian shares.

Broker-assisted: Add $10 per trade; flat rate for equity trades up to 5000 shares + $.01/share for additional shares over 5000.

Options: $24 + $1/contract per trade, any price.

SUPPORT SYSTEMS: 1-888-597-6840. Trading demo, standard glossary, e-mail. Links to Reuters, Big Charts, NewsAlert, Briefing.com, Zacks, EDGAR Online.

Request forms, apply by mail, to open new account.

OPERATIONAL SYSTEMS: Standard.

BACKGROUND INFORMATION: CompuTel Securities, member NASD/SIPC, is a division of Thomas F. White & Co., Inc.

CRESTAR INVESTMENT GROUP

URL: www.crestarinvest.com

TYPE OF SITE: Full service brokerage firm.

USERS: Online traders, plus touch-tone.

SNAIL MAIL: Attn: Internet Department
11 S. Tenth Street
Richmond, VA 23219

PHONE: 1-800-CRESTAR (273-7827)

E-MAIL: crc@crestarinvest.com

SERVICES: TouchTone Invest™ to access account status and quotes, and trade 24 hours.

EXECUTION SYSTEMS: National Financial Services Corporation (a subsidiary of Fidelity Investments) is the clearing agent.

FEES:

Account minimum: Monies reside in CrestFund® Money Market fund. Free dividend reinvestment.

Limit/market trades: 10% discount off normal commissions.

Broker-assisted: 1-800-368-5003. Minimum commission $40. $38 + .5% of principal per trade totaling up to $15,000. $38 + .45% of principal per trade totaling $15,000–$25,000. $40 + .4% of principal per trade totaling $25,000–$50,000. $40 + .3% of principal per trade totaling $50,000 and greater.

Mutual funds: $50/trade for no-loads.

Options: Minimum commission $40. $38 + .9% of principal per trade totaling up to $3000. $38 + .8% of principal per trade totaling $3000–$10,000. $38 + .7% of principal per trade totaling $10,000 and greater.

Bonds: Corporate—$4 per $1000 face value, minimum $40 per transaction.

Margin: Minimum equity $5000; brokers call plus .75% to 2%.

APPEALING FEATURES: Online banking.

SUPPORT SYSTEMS: Toll-free number and e-mail. Access to earnings estimates, stock and industry reports, news.

OPERATIONAL SYSTEMS: Standard hardware plus Netscape Navigator 3.0 Gold or higher U.S. 128-bit encrypted version, or Microsoft Internet Explorer 3.0 or higher U.S. 128-bit encrypted version, and Acrobat Reader from Adobe Systems.

BACKGROUND INFORMATION: Crestar Investment Group, member SIPC, NASD, is affiliated with Crestar Bank.

DATEK ONLINE HOLDINGS CORP.

URL: www.datek.com

TYPE OF SITE: Full service online brokerage. Web TV compatible. No options, AON orders, BB, or Canadian stock trading. Stop orders for Nasdaq only. Will trade listed or Nasdaq penny stocks.

USERS: All levels of online traders. Not licensed for business in ND or ID. Foreign accounts accepted.

SNAIL MAIL: 100 Wood Avenue South
Iselin, NJ 08830-2716

PHONE: 1-888-GO-DATEK (463-2835)

SERVICES: Free real-time quotes for Nasdaq, NYSE, and AMEX, as well as instantly updated account information. Beta testing in development for real-time dynamically updated quotes ($20/month subscription fee to securities industry or legal entity accounts). New product, Streamer, offers free *streaming* real-time quotes with a Java applet. Level II Nasdaq quotes promised. Current portfolio with order status updated throughout the day. Confirmation (checkpoint) page; daily activity page.

EXECUTION SYSTEMS: Access to Island ECN. Customers can go directly to https://orders2.datek.com (or orders3 through orders11). Cleared through Datek Online Clearing Corp., member NASD/SIPC.

FEES:
Account minimum: $2000.
Limit/market trades: With TradeNow™ button, $9.99 for up to (and for each) 5000 shares. Free if not executed in 1 minute—conditions and restrictions apply. (One free trade for birthday.)
Broker-assisted: $25 ($9.99 if computer system is down).
Mutual funds: 3000+ to choose from at $9.99. Quotes and research available on 10,000+ funds.
IRA accounts: $40 annual fee; $25 setup; $60 closing.
Margin: Brokers call less ¼% (subject to change).

APPEALING FEATURES: Sophisticated help desk integrated into all site services. Fast quote icon.

SUPPORT SYSTEMS: Toll-free numbers and e-mail. Free charts, news, and research. Glossary; integrated help desk.

OPERATING SYSTEMS: Standard.

BACKGROUND INFORMATION: Datek Online Holdings Corporation (Datek Online) was formed through the January 1998 merger of Datek Securities Corporation and its technology provider BigThink, a researcher and developer of financial services software.

DISCOVER BROKERAGE DIRECT INC.

URL: www.discoverbrokerage.com

TYPE OF SITE: Full service brokerage offering trading online, by touch-tone, and by broker.

USERS: All levels of online investors.

SNAIL MAIL: 333 Market Street, 25th Floor
San Francisco, CA 94105-3407

PHONE: 1-800-58-INVEST (584-6837)

E-MAIL: clientsupport@discoverbrokerage.com

SERVICES: Download data into Quicken and Money. Pager service promised. Personalized home page; checkpoint page to review and validate orders; confirmation page to place order and receive confirmation number.

FEES:

Account minimum: $2000, no maintenance fee. Receive $75 credit upon account activation with online application. Free dividend reinvestment. Alliance Money Market account, $12 annual fee with free sweep.

Quotes: Delayed quotes and info available before log-in; unlimited real-time quotes available upon log-in during market hours.

Limit trades: Listed—$19.95 for up to 5000 shares, then $.01/share for entire order. OTC—$19.95 for any number of shares.

Market: Listed—$14.95 for up to 5000 shares, then $.01/share for entire order. OTC—$14.95 for any number of shares.

Blue Chip Basket: 10 stocks for $39.95.

Touch-tone: InstaTrade includes 100 free quotes per trade; fees same as online.

Broker-assisted: 1-800-825-5873. Listed—$.02/share, $34 minimum, $100 for 5000 shares. OTC—$.015/share, $34 minimum, $75 for 5000 shares.

Penny stocks: $25 + 2.75% of principal; $300 for 20,000 shares @ $.50.

Mutual funds: 4000 funds to choose from at $25; 237+ have no fee.

Options: $25 + 2.75% of principal; check with broker for specific transaction fees.

IRA accounts: Free and setup free; $50 closing. No options trading; covered calls only.

Treasuries/bonds: Check with broker for specific transaction fees.

Margin: Brokers call plus ¾% to 2.5%, based on declining balance.

APPEALING FEATURES: Blue Chip Basket enables purchase of 10 stocks for $39.95.

SUPPORT SYSTEMS: 1-800-688-6896 for customer support. E-mail, standard demo and glossary, commission calculator. Free Zacks, Thomson Investor historical company information, and institutional equity research reports. Subscription research through Equity Research service, customized monthly and with e-mail alerts of report updates. Available on subscription at $4.95/month or $49.95/year for one stock, $9.95/month or $99.95/year for 5 stocks, $14.95/month or $149.95/year for 10 stocks, $19.95/month or $199.95/year for 20 stocks, and $34.95/month or $349.95/year for 40 stocks; free with account balance of over $100,000.

OPERATIONAL SYSTEMS: Standard, plus Adobe Acrobat software.

BACKGROUND INFORMATION: In August 1995, Discover Brokerage Direct (then known as Lombard Brokerage, Inc.) became one of the first financial institutions to offer investing over the Internet. In January 1997, Lombard Brokerage, Inc. was acquired by Dean Witter, Discover & Co. and renamed Discover Brokerage Direct. In May 1997, Dean Witter, Discover & Co. merged with Morgan Stanley Group Inc., creating Morgan Stanley Dean Witter & Co.

EMPIRE FINANCIAL GROUP INC.

URL: www.lowfees.com

TYPE OF SITE: Full service discount brokerage.

USERS: All levels of online investors.

SNAIL MAIL: 2170 W. State Road 434, Suite 124
Longwood, FL 32779

PHONE: 1-877-569-3337

E-MAIL: empire1@sprintmail.com

SERVICES: All trades and products.

EXECUTION SYSTEMS: Advantage Trading Group, Inc. is the clearing agent. Sells order flow.

FEES:

Account minimum: None. $2000 for margin account.

Quotes: Real-time quotes at $14.95/month for listed or OTC, plus $.05/quote, minus 250 free quotes, minus 25 free quotes per exe-cuted online transaction.

Limit trades: Listed—$11.95 for up to 5000 shares, then $.01/share for entire order. Nasdaq—$11.95. Add $3/trade for postage/handling fee.

Market trades: Listed—$6.95 for up to 5000 shares, then $.01/share for entire order. Nasdaq—$6.95. Add $3/trade for postage/han-dling fee. First 5 market trades free on sign-up.

Broker-assisted: 1-800-569-3337. $22 (includes $3 fee) for limit or-ders. Listed—+ $.02/share for entire order. Nasdaq—+ $.01/share for entire order. No commission rates for short sales.

Penny stocks: $22 (includes $3 fee) + 3% of principal (e.g., $322 for 20,000 shares @ $.50).

Foreign: $.03/share ($40 minimum for Canadian; $125 minimum for other foreign).

Mutual funds: $25/trade.

IRA accounts: $25 setup, $75 closing; $50 annual fee waived with $10,000 account and 4+ trades per year.

Options: $25 + $1.95/contract.

Margin: Brokers call less 1% to plus 2%.

APPEALING FEATURES: Free market trades; IPO center; online application form.

SUPPORT SYSTEMS: Toll-free number during business hours; otherwise, 1-407-702-0258. Pager service (minimum 25 trades per month) for alerts.

OPERATIONAL SYSTEMS: Standard.

BACKGROUND INFORMATION: Lowfees.com is currently the online trading site of Empire Financial Group, Inc., a member of NASD/SIPC, MSRB, and SIC. Empire is in the process of changing its URL to www.Empirenow.com.

FAR SIGHT FINANCIAL SERVICES LP

URL: www.farsight.com

TYPE OF SITE: Online brokerage firm.

USERS: Online investors needing little or no assistance.

SNAIL MAIL: 201 Broadway
Cambridge, MA 02139

PHONE: 1-800-830-7483

E-MAIL: service@farsight.com

SERVICES: Integrated Online Personal Finance^{sm} is the pilot program for comprehensive integration of checking, investing, bill paying, and advanced management tools into a single convenient online service. Site security is major focus, with detailed entry instructions and automatic log-out within 30 minutes of last click.

EXECUTION SYSTEMS: Clearing broker is National Financial Services Corporation.

FEES:

Account minimum: None to open cash account; funds must be received prior to settlement. $5000 minimum for margin account. On account approval, you may be able to place an order immediately for stock trading at a minimum of $5/share, up to an aggregate of $10,000 or your trade limit, whichever is greater. First transaction cannot be a margin purchase. FarSight reserves the right to qualify approval through a customer credit check.

Quotes: 200 free real-time quotes with account activation, plus 100 free with each trade. Buy additional quotes at $10 for 200, $20 for 500, $30 for 1000.

Trades: First trade commission-free up to $10,000. Then $20 flat fee per trade of up to 1000 shares, plus $.01/share over 1000. For shares valued at less than $1, minimum $20/trade, maximum 5% of principal. No postage/handling fees.

Mutual funds: 5000 mutual funds to choose from, including 650 no-load, no fee. Otherwise, $35 each where applicable.

Margin: Brokers call plus up to 2%.

APPEALING FEATURES: Online help site navigation tutorial.

SUPPORT SYSTEMS: Integrated glossary and help for every page. Toll-free and e-mail customer service. Personal home page, news, symbol search, time and sales, market indices, basic company info from Nelsons, Media General, Baseline, customized charts, hot list of 100 securities, real-time alerts.

Open account by e-mailing online application.

OPERATIONAL SYSTEMS:

CPU: Pentium-based processor.

Memory: 32MB RAM.

Modem: 64/128k ISDN, 56v90 or 33.6v90 kbps.

Operating system: Win95/98 or NT 4.0 workstation.

Browser: Microsoft Explorer 3.0 or Netscape Navigator 3.0.

BACKGROUND INFORMATION: FarSight Financial Services LP, member SIPC, was funded and organized in 1995 by D.E. Shaw & Co. LP to provide retail online financial services. D.E. Shaw & Co. LP is a global securities and investment firm founded in 1988.

FIDELITY INVESTMENTS

URL: www.fidelity.com

TYPE OF SITE: Full service brokerage, including online, touch-tone and electronic trading.

USERS: All levels of investors, with discount for high minimum balance and trade frequency.

SNAIL MAIL: P.O. Box 193
Boston, MA 02101-0193

PHONE: 1-800-544-6666

E-MAIL: Directly through site icons.

SERVICES: Place orders through two-way pager or PDA. InstantBroker® (for active trader accounts) permits up to 30 securities quoted every 15 minutes with a maximum of 100 quotes per day. Quotes are available for stocks, mutual funds, indices, and options. Price triggers and execution reports delivered to pager, PDA, or e-mail. Summary of account balances as of previous day's close and current account positions at a specific time. Automatic notification of margin call. Asset allocation planner and investment growth calculator.

EXECUTION SYSTEMS: Clearing company is National Financial Services Corporation, a Fidelity Investments company.

FEES:

Account minimum: None for Fidelity Online Trading.

Quotes: Delayed quotes available for up to 30 securities, to a maximum of 100 quote reports per day. Real-time quotes available on subscription.

Trades: For qualifying accounts of active traders (maintaining a minimum $20,000 balance and making between 36 and 72 trades per year), the base rate per trade is $14.95 for electronic orders. Otherwise, for stock trades placed via Fidelity Online Trading, the base rate is $25/trade, up to 1000 shares. Over 1000, add $.02/share for entire order. Maximum is 5% of principal. Limit/stop orders, $5 premium per transaction.

TouchTone Xpress®: 1-800-544-5555. 35% off broker rates. Premium for limit/stop orders is applied after the discount.

Broker-assisted: Minimum $59 for up to 100 shares, $85 + $.14/share for 101–500 shares, $95 + $.07/share for 501–1000 shares, $110 + $.05/share for 1001–2000 shares, $125 + $.025/share for 2001 shares and up. Maximum is 5% of principal. Limit/stop orders, $5 premium per transaction.

Mutual funds: No charge for most Fidelity funds; may be subject to redemption, exchange, or sales charge. $28.95 online fee for non-Fidelity funds. For broker assistance, a base fee of $35 plus a percentage of the transaction with a maximum fee of $150 per transaction. For touch-tone, 20% off broker fees, minimum of $30.

Options: Touch-tone—20% off broker rates. Online—25% off broker rates. Broker, $28.75 + 1.6% of principal for transactions up to $2500; $48.75 + .80% of principal for transactions from $2501–$10,000; $98.75 + .30% of principal for transactions over $10,000. Minimum is $34.25 + $1.75/contract (minimum of $36 and not to exceed maximum of $36 per contract for the first two contracts, + $4/contract thereafter; or one-half of the principal amount, whichever is less).

Bonds: Corporate—as agent, $36 + $4/bond up to 25 bonds, plus $3/bond over 25.

Treasuries: $50 for orders of 20 bonds or fewer. No charge over 20 bonds. $50 service fee for all Treasury auction and T-bill trades.

UITs: Minimum charge of $35; service charge at redemption.

Precious metals: Minimum charge of $44. Percentage charged on gross amount: .99% up to 2.9% on buys totaling $100,000 down to $0; .75% up to 2% on sells totaling $250,000 down to $0.

Margin: Brokers call less .25% to plus 2%.

APPEALING FEATURES: Commission calculator—critical for translating commission schedules.

SUPPORT SYSTEMS: Toll-free number and e-mail; extensive FAQs and glossary. Demo of company profile report and sample of first call earnings estimates. Research/news includes market snapshot, charts, news,

Reuters, indexes, calendars of offerings, Fidelity's online magazine, mutual fund reviews, stock evaluator and company profiles, annuity reviews, and Salomon Smith Barney research.

OPERATIONAL SYSTEMS: Standard hardware plus version 4.0 or higher of either Netscape Communicator or Microsoft Internet Explorer. JavaScript, Java. Color configuration and screen resolution in 256 colors, 800×600 dpi minimum. Plug-ins. For printing and viewing, Adobe Acrobat; for audio and video, Microsoft® Media Player.

BACKGROUND INFORMATION: Fidelity, member NYSE/SIPC, was founded in 1946 by Edward C. Johnson II.

1ST-DISCOUNT BROKERAGE, INC.

URL: www.1st-discount.com

TYPE OF SITE: International, full-service online trading firm.

USERS: Online traders; foreign accounts accepted. No stop orders or bonds.

SNAIL MAIL: 5883 Lake Worth Road
                Lake Worth, FL 33463

PHONE: 1-888-642-2811

E-MAIL: webmaster@1st-discount.com

SERVICES: Full brokerage.

EXECUTION SYSTEMS: All transactions cleared through U.S. Clearing, a division of Fleet Securities, Inc.

FEES:

Account minimum: None.

Quotes: Unlimited delayed quotes. $29.95/month subscription to real-time quotes.

Limit/market trades: $14.75/order up to 5000 shares, plus $3.50 postage/handling fee.

Touch-tone: $24.95/order.

Mutual funds: $35/transaction for no load.

Options: $25 + $1.75/contract; minimum $30/transaction.

APPEALING FEATURES: Free portfolio tracker through Reality Online; site offered in English, Spanish, and German.

SUPPORT SYSTEMS: Toll-free number for customer support. Standard glossary and FAQs, demo.

Open account by online application.

OPERATIONAL SYSTEMS: Standard.

BACKGROUND INFORMATION: 1st Discount Brokerage is a member of NASD/SIPC.

FIRST TRADE SECURITIES, INC.

URL: www.firstrade.com

TYPE OF SITE: Full service online brokerage offering touch-tone trading. No Canadian stocks.

USERS: Online traders; foreign accounts accepted.

SNAIL MAIL: 136-21 Roosevelt Avenue, 3rd Floor
          Flushing, NY 11354

PHONE: 1-800-869-8800

E-MAIL: webmaster@firstrade.com

SERVICES: Touch-tone orders can be placed by MarketTouch, 1-800-362-6275; service includes real-time quotes, stock and option trades, account balances, and positions at same prices as Internet.

EXECUTION SYSTEMS: Orders routed through broker approval. Clearing agent is U.S. Clearing Corp.

FEES:

Account minimum: None. $2000 for margin account. 3.5% interest paid on credit balances.

Quotes: 100 real-time quotes available per order. Traders may subscribe to DTN.IQ streaming real-time data and portfolio management for $50 initiation fee, $79/month + exchange fees. One week free trial. No postage, handling or other hidden fees on trades.

Trades: Listed (limit/market)—$9.95/trade for any number of shares (except penny stocks). Multiple charges for multiple executions plus $1.50 for each extra trade; use AON on large orders. Nasdaq (market)—$4.95/trade of 1000+ shares (except BB stocks).

Broker-assisted: 1-800-825-5873. $29.95 for any number of shares.

Mutual funds: No-load funds, $25; broker-assisted, $50.

Options: $20 + $1.75/contract (minimum $29); broker-assisted, add $10/transaction (minimum $35).

IRA accounts: Free.

Margin: Brokers call less ½ to 1%, based on balance.

APPEALING FEATURES: Very low margin rates. Free browser CD-ROM.

SUPPORT SYSTEMS: 1-888-988-6168 for customer support. E-mail, extensive glossary, demo. Quick.Nav for easy site accessibility. High-speed backup connections and excess capacity to handle activity increase; fully functional redundant backup in case of emergency. Research includes market summaries and news through Reality Online, delayed quotes, and investment objective listing (mutual funds). Account reports include portfolio page showing holdings, balances, executions; checkpoint page to review, edit, and validate orders; confirmation page to acknowledge order and give confirmation number.

Open account by secure online application. Possible to trade in one business day.

OPERATIONAL SYSTEMS: Standard.

BACKGROUND INFORMATION: First Trade Securities, Inc., member NASD/SIPC, was founded in 1985 as First Flushing Securities and is now a wholly-owned subsidiary of Quick & Reilly Group, Inc.

R.J. FORBES GROUP, INC.

URL: www.forbesnet.com

TYPE OF SITE: Discount brokerage site offering online and touch-tone trading.

USERS: All levels of online traders. Foreign accounts accepted—cash only.

SNAIL MAIL: 8 Fletcher Place
             Melville, NY 11747

PHONE: 1-800-488-0090

SERVICES: Portfolio, confirmation, and daily activity reports through Reality Online, a Reuters company.

EXECUTION SYSTEMS: Clearing company is U.S. Clearing Corp.

FEES:

Account minimum: $5000.

Quotes: Unlimited real-time online quotes for $29.95/month. Free on touch-tone orders.

Limit/market trades: $9.95 for up to 5000 shares, then add $.01/share for entire order (e.g., $109.95 for 10,000 shares).

Broker-assisted: Add $35 ($44.95 for any number of shares).

BB and penny stocks: Online fees same as broker-assisted. BB must be ordered through broker.

Canadian stocks: $.015/share; $35 minimum.

Mutual funds: $50/trade.

Options: Internet or touch-tone—$40 + $1–$4/contract.

IRA accounts: Free; free setup; closing $50.

Margin: Brokers call plus .75% to 2%.

SUPPORT SYSTEMS: Toll-free number. Glossary. Screen views through Reality Online. Research/news includes Zacks, company news.

OPERATIONAL SYSTEMS: Standard.

BACKGROUND INFORMATION: R.J. Forbes Group is a member NASD/SIPC and MSRB.

FREEDOM INVESTMENTS, INC.

URL: www.freedominvestments.com

TYPE OF SITE: Discount online brokerage, also offering touch-tone and PC trading.

USERS: All levels of online investors.

SNAIL MAIL: 11422 Miracle Hills Drive, Suite 501
Omaha, NE 68154

PHONE: 1-800-944-4033

SERVICES: Orders may be made via touch-tone, PC via modem or Internet, or broker.

FEES:

Account minimum: $2000. Currently offering free securities trading (listed and Nasdaq/OTC stocks with minimum value of $5/share and minimum transaction value of $500) for 30 days with new account. Call 1-800-381-1481 to verify and for information.

Quotes: 15 minutes of free real-time quotes on opening account; additional 4 minutes per trade; otherwise, $.25/minute.

Limit/market trades: Internet—$15 flat, any size, price, or type of order. Touch-tone or PC—$25 flat, any size, price, or type of order.

Broker-assisted: $.03/share, subject to a $45 minimum (e.g., $150 for 5000 shares).

Penny/Canadian/foreign stocks: Must have valid Nasdaq symbol. Fees same as broker-assisted.

Mutual funds: Call for more information.

Bonds: $5/bond, minimum $40.

Options: Internet, PC, or touch-tone—$45 + $2/contract. Broker—$50 + $3.50/contract.

IRA accounts: $25/year.

Margin: Brokers call plus 1½% to 2%.

APPEALING FEATURES: Free Trade Flash software.

SUPPORT SYSTEMS: Toll-free numbers.

OPERATIONAL SYSTEMS: Standard.

BACKGROUND INFORMATION: Freedom Investments, Inc. (member NYSE, NASD, and SIPC) started in 1994 and is a wholly-owned subsidiary of Fahnestock & Co.

FREEMAN WELWOOD

URL: www.freemanwelwood.com

TYPE OF SITE: Discount brokerage offering online, touch-tone, and broker-assisted trading.

USERS: All levels of online investors.

SNAIL MAIL: P.O. Box 21886
             Seattle, WA 98111

PHONE: 1-800-729-7585

SERVICES: Standard portfolio management reports.

FEES:

Account minimum: None. Free dividend reinvestment.

Quotes: 100 free real-time quotes per trade; free by touch-tone.

Trades: Limit—$19.95 up to 1000 shares; then $.01/share for additional (e.g., $59.95 for 5000 shares). Market—$14.95 up to 1000 shares; then $.01/share for additional.

Touch-tone: 10% off standard pricing.

Broker-assisted: $34 + $.05/share for up to 800 shares; then $.025/share (e.g., $39 for 100 shares; $179 for 5000 shares).

Penny stocks: $34 + .025% of dollar amount (e.g., $284 for 20,000 shares @ $.50).

Mutual funds: 2000 to choose from. 250+ free no-load funds; others, 10% off standard pricing. $34/trade + $.001 of principal + $25 for redemption or exchanges.

IRA accounts: Free with $10,000 account or one trade per year; setup free; closing $25.

Options: 10% off standard pricing. $34 + $2.50/contract with broker.

Bonds: $34/trade + $2.50/bond with broker only.

Treasuries: $50/trade with broker only.

Margin: Brokers call plus ½% to 2%.

SUPPORT SERVICES: 1-800-693-9311 Mon–Fri, 6am–9pm; Sat, 8am–1pm. Standard demo and glossary; news and research. Ten office locations.

OPERATIONAL SYSTEMS: Standard.

BACKGROUND INFORMATION: Privately held company, founded in 1972 as one of the first discount brokerages.

GAY FINANCIAL NETWORK INVESTMENTS

URL: www.gfn.com

TYPE OF SITE: Discount online brokerage.

USERS: Online traders.

SNAIL MAIL: 111 Broadway
New York, NY 10006

PHONE: 1-800-354-7429

SERVICES: Caters to gay clientele, providing news, legal services, and links to related topics.

EXECUTION SYSTEMS: Through FarSight Financial Services.

FEES:

Account minimum: None; $5000 for margin. Accounts may settle "trade + 3" for equities or "next day" for options; may be restricted to "cash on hand" for mutual funds, IRAs, and stocks at less than $5/share.

Quotes: Unlimited delayed.

Limit/market trades: $19.95 up to 1000 shares; then $.02/share additional ($99.95 for 5000 shares).

Broker-assisted: Through FarSight Financial Services.

Margin: Brokers call plus ½% to 2%.

SUPPORT SYSTEMS: Toll-free number. Full service news site, including legal advice.

OPERATIONAL SYSTEMS: Standard.

BACKGROUND INFORMATION: Gay Financial Network Investments is a division of FarSight Financial Services LP.

INTERNET TRADING.COM

URL: www.internettrading.com

TYPE OF SITE: Online discount brokerage with Internet, touch-tone, or direct dial-up software trading access.

USERS: All levels of online traders; check for registration in your state.

SNAIL MAIL: National Service Center
100 Bush Street, Suite 1000
San Francisco, CA 94104

PHONE: 1-800-696-2811

E-MAIL: webmaster@internettrading.com

SERVICES: Dynamic portfolio management reports, charts, research.

FEES:
Account minimum: $10,000; $25 annual inactivity fee.
Quotes: Unlimited delayed quotes. Real-time quotes available.
Limit/market trades: OTC—$14/trade. Listed—$17.50 (includes $3.50 fee) for up to 5000 shares; over 5000 shares, $.0175/share for entire order (e.g., $91.02 for 5001 shares).
Touch-tone: Same fees as online.
Broker-assisted: $6 extra.
Mutual funds: Available through broker.
Options: $17.50 (includes $3.50 fee) + $2/contract.
IRA accounts: $40/year; setup $25.
Margin: $8\frac{3}{4}$% to $10\frac{1}{2}$%.

APPEALING FEATURES: Ask-A-Broker e-mail available to nonclients. Real-time account updating.

SUPPORT SYSTEMS: 1-800-696-2811, 9am–7pm EST. Online trading demo. FAQs.
Download forms to open account.

OPERATIONAL SYSTEMS: Direct dial-up software requires minimum 386 PC with 2MB RAM running Windows 3.1 or later, with a Hayes-compatible modem.

BACKGROUND INFORMATION: Internet Trading.com is a division of Emmett A. Larkin Company, Inc., a full service brokerage founded in 1959, member NASD, Chicago Stock Exchange, MSRB, SIPC.

INVESTEX SECURITIES GROUP, INC.

URL: www.investexpress.com

TYPE OF SITE: Full service brokerage with online trading. Web TV compatible.

USERS: All levels of online investors.

SNAIL MAIL: 50 Broad Street
New York, NY 10004

PHONE: 1-800-392-7192

SERVICES: Monthly statements; online trades confirmed immediately on execution with written confirmation; phone confirmation on touch-tone trades. Portfolio pages to trade and view balances, value of positions, status of daily orders. Checkpoint page to review order before sending.

EXECUTION SYSTEMS: Clearing firm is National Financial Services Corporation, a Fidelity Investments company.

FEES:

Account minimum: None; $5000 margin. Automatic cash sweeps into margin or money market account. No postage/handling charge on Internet equity/option trades.

Quotes: Unlimited delayed quotes; $14/month for dynamic real-time quote system.

Limit trades: Listed—$17.95 up to 4999 shares; then add $.005/share for entire order (e.g., $67.95 for 10,000 shares). OTC—$17.95 for any number of shares.

Market trades: Listed—$13.95 up to 4999 shares; then add $.005/share for entire order (e.g., $63.95 for 10,000 shares). OTC—$13.95 for any number of shares.

Broker-assisted: $30 + $3.50 postage/handling fee per trade up to 500 shares; $33 + $3.50 postage/handling fee per trade for 501–1650 shares; then $.02/share. IRAs and foreign stocks available.

Mutual funds: 2000 to choose from. Load funds, minimum order $2500; no fee. No-load funds up to $6500, $45 per trade; over $6500, $65 per trade. Redemptions/exchanges, $35/trade.

Options: $20 + $1.75/contract through online. $25 + $2.50/contract through broker.

Bonds: Municipal and zero coupon—$5/bond, minimum $50. Corporate—$5/bond, minimum $40. No charge for UITs.

CDs: $5/$1000; minimum $50/trade.

Precious metals: 2% of principal amount; minimum $75/trade.

Treasuries: $5/bond; minimum $50/trade.

Margin: Brokers call plus ¾% to 2%.

SUPPORT SYSTEMS: Toll-free numbers. Demo. Research includes 24-hour news, business headlines, USAToday MoneyLine, Hoover's Online company reports, Reuters, Thomson's MarketEdge.

OPERATIONAL SYSTEMS: Standard.

BACKGROUND INFORMATION: Investex Securities Group, Inc., established in 1992, is a full service brokerage.

INVESTRADE, INC.

URL: www.investrade.com

TYPE OF SITE: Discount brokerage with online, touch-tone, PDA, and broker-assisted trading.

USERS: All levels of online investors; no foreign accounts; no non-US stocks.

SNAIL MAIL: 950 N. Milwaukee Avenue, Suite 102
Glenview, IL 60025

PHONE: 1-800-498-7120

SERVICES: Portfolio management report, confirmation page, daily activity reports. BB, pink sheet, and bond orders require broker assistance.

EXECUTION SYSTEMS: Clearing company is BHC Securities.

FEES:

Account minimum: $2000. Balances can be swept into money market account.

Quotes: 100 free real-time quotes on opening account; additional 50/trade. Unlimited delayed quotes.

Trades: Limit—$11.95 for any trade. Market—$7.95 for any trade.

Touch-tone: QuickTel® proprietary service, 1-800-498-7120. Same fees as online trades.

Broker-assisted: $26.95 on limit orders; $22.95 on market orders. BB/pink sheet—$27.95 for shares at $2+. Stop orders on Nasdaq only.

Penny stocks: $29 for any trade less than $2/share.

Mutual funds: $29/trade. 3800+ to choose from, including 600+ no-loads at no fee.

IRA accounts: No annual; free setup; $50 closing.

Options: $1.75/contract, $14.95 minimum. No naked calls; naked puts require $50,000 margin equity.

Margin: Brokers call less 1% to plus 1.5%.

SUPPORT SYSTEMS: 1-800-498-7120 for customer service. E-mail, demo. page views, standard glossary. Amazon.com affiliate bookstore.

Comprehensive FAQs section. Research includes market indices, fundamentals and historical information, news headlines.

OPERATIONAL SYSTEMS: Standard.

BACKGROUND INFORMATION: Investrade, Inc. is a division of Regal Discount Securities.

J.B. OXFORD & COMPANY

URL: www.jboxford.com

TYPE OF SITE: Full service discount brokerage.

USERS: Online investors, all levels. Foreign accounts accepted.

SNAIL MAIL: 9665 Wilshire Boulevard, 3rd Floor
Beverly Hills, CA 90212

PHONE: 1-800-500-5007

E-MAIL: custsvc@jboc.com (plus directory)

SERVICES: Trading through Oxford Trading Desk for order taking only. Portfolio manager hyperlinks to charts, quotes, news stories relating to positions held. Trade status and history.

EXECUTION SYSTEMS: Self-clearing.

FEES:

Account minimum: $2000.

Quotes: Real-time quotes available through PCQuote (100/trade by touch-tone; subscription online). Symbol wizard.

Market trades: $10 + $3 fee, for up to 3000 shares; then add $.01/share for entire order.

Limit/stop trades: $15 + $3 fee, for up to 3000 shares; then add $.01/share for entire order. *No stop orders on Nasdaq.*

NetTrade Account: Maintain $250,000+ equity; trades of 1000–5000 shares, $5+/share only. Market trades via personal broker, $12 + $3 fee; online, $10 + $3 fee. Limit trades add $5.

Telephone Trader: $2 extra per order.

Oxford Trader: 1-800-782-1876. Order taking only—$8 extra per order.

Broker-assisted: $12 extra per order.

Mutual funds: No-load fund, $20. $25 for broker-assisted.

Options: $25 + $3 fee, plus $2.50/contract. $35 + $3 fee + $2.75/contract for broker-assisted.

Bonds: Listed—$5/bond; $40 minimum.

Penny stocks: $.03/share or 5% of principal, whichever is less; $25 minimum.

Margin: Brokers call less .25% to plus 2.75%.

APPEALING FEATURES: "Widgets"—loan rate, calculator, and retirement planning.

SUPPORT SYSTEMS: 1-800-944-3295, 9am–6pm EST. Voice mail and e-mail. Glossary, demo, site help. Research/news includes Argus daily reports, MarketEdge Weekly Second Opinion, News Alert.

OPERATIONAL SYSTEMS: Standard.

BACKGROUND INFORMATION: J.B. Oxford & Company, member NASD, was founded in 1994 and is a wholly-owned subsidiary of publicly traded JB Oxford Holdings, Inc.

MAIN STREET MARKET

URL: www.mainstmarket.com

TYPE OF SITE: Discount online brokerage.

USERS: All levels of online traders.

SNAIL MAIL: U.S. Clearing
                Attn: Brokerage Services
                26 Broadway, 12th Floor
                New York, NY 10004-1798

PHONE: 1-800-710-7160

SERVICES: Real-time quote system from Reality Online, with symbol lookup. Online trades confirmed immediately on execution plus written confirmation; monthly summary includes portfolio evaluation and tax statement.

EXECUTION SYSTEMS: Clearing company is U.S. Clearing, a division of Fleet Securities.

FEES:
Account minimum: None. Free dividend reinvestment.
Limit trades: $19.95 up to 1000 shares; then $.02/share over 1000.
Market trades: $14.95 up to 1000 shares; then $.02/share over 1000.
Options: $35 + .009% of principal for transactions $3000 and less; $35 + .008% of principal for transactions $3001–$10,000; $35 + .007% of principal for transactions over $10,000. $25/contract maximum and $3/contract minimum.
Bonds: $30/trade through broker.
Treasuries: $40/trade (auction only) through broker.

SUPPORT SYSTEMS: Toll-free number. Demo, glossary, FAQ section.

OPERATIONAL SYSTEMS: Standard.

BACKGROUND INFORMATION: Main Street Market is a discounted online trading service of the Brokerage Service Division of U.S. Clearing.

MYDISCOUNTBROKER.COM
(SOVEREIGN SECURITIES)

URL: www.mydiscountbroker.com

TYPE OF SITE: Full service brokerage offering discounted online and desktop trading.

USERS: All levels of online traders. Foreign accounts accepted. No margins. Web TV and MacIntosh compatible.

SNAIL MAIL: 1201 Elm Street, Suite 121
Dallas, TX 75270

PHONE: 1-888-882-5600

E-MAIL: service@mydiscountbroker.com

SERVICES: Immediate account updating, telephone confirmations on request, financial planner. Offers IPOs through Wit Capital Group.

EXECUTION SYSTEMS: Clearing company is Southwest Securities Group.

FEES:

Account minimum: None. $2000 for margin account. Free dividend reinvestment.

Quotes: Unlimited free real-time quotes.

Limit/market trades: $12 up to 5000 shares; then add $.01/share for entire order.

Broker-assisted: $25 minimum for up to 1000 shares; $35 for 1001–2500 shares; $45 for 2501–5000 shares; add $.02/share for over 5000 shares.

Penny stocks: 5% of principal; $21.25 minimum (e.g., $500 for 20,000 shares @ $.50).

Mutual funds: $25/trade + .0015% of principal + $1.25 postage/handling fee for no-loads. For front-end funds, the load fee is subject to a minimum of the above.

Options: $12 + $2/contract. Broker-assisted rates are $25 + $2/contract; minimum $35.

IRA accounts: No annual fee or setup; closing $25.

Margin: Brokers call plus 1.25%.

APPEALING FEATURES: Free Investor View order entry and portfolio management software.

SUPPORT SYSTEMS: Toll-free number. Standard glossary, demo, limited charts and information, newsletter.

OPERATIONAL SYSTEMS: Standard.

BACKGROUND INFORMATION: Formerly Sovereign Securities, a traditional discount brokerage begun in 1996, Mydiscountbroker.com, member NASC, is a wholly-owned subsidiary of Southwest Securities Group, Inc.

NATIONAL DISCOUNT BROKERS, INC.

URL: www.ndb.com

TYPE OF SITE: Discount brokerage service. Stocks/options only; no margins or short sales online.

USERS: All levels of online investors. Foreign accounts accepted.

SNAIL MAIL: 7 Hanover Square, 4th Floor
New York, NY 10004

PHONE: 1-800-888-3999

E-MAIL: help@ndb.com

SERVICES: WebStation (online) and PowerBroker (touch-tone) accept only stock/option trades. All others securities are traded through broker. Portfolio lists open orders for cancellation, account value and balances, order execution history, transaction history. Confirmations by e-mail. Monthly statements and confirmations by mail.

EXECUTION SYSTEMS: All securities are offered through Sherwood Securities Corp., a proprietary trading firm since 1968 and a registered specialist on the American Stock Exchange.

FEES:

Account minimum: $2000. Free asset management account ProCash Plus. Free dividend reinvestment and automatic sweep of cash into Alliance Money Market funds. Unlimited same-day trades on the same side of a given issue available for a single transaction fee. Add $.01/share if greater than 5000 shares total.

Quotes: 100 free real-time quotes per trade (via touch-tone only), symbol lookup. Create 3 customized quote lists.

Limit trades: (WebStation online) Listed—$19.75 up to 5000 shares; then add .01/share for entire order. OTC—$19.75 for any number of shares.

Market trades: (WebStation online) Listed—$14.75 up to 5000 shares; then add .01/share for entire order. OTC—$14.75 for any number of shares.

Touch-tone: (PowerBroker) $19.95 market, $22.95 limit, for up to 5000 shares; then add $.01/share for entire order.

Broker-assisted: $24.95 market, $27.95 limit, for up to 5000 shares; then add $.01/share for entire order.

Foreign stocks: Canadian—$30 + $.02/share. Other—$125 + $.02/share.

Mutual funds: 6000+ to choose from, including 700+ no-loads with no fees.

Options: $35 + $2.50/contract (not yet available online).

IRA accounts: Free with $10,000+ account; otherwise, $35/year.

Margin: Brokers call plus up to 2%.

APPEALING FEATURES: Rapid Research Line provides the latest historical and investment information reports, delivered 24 hours daily to any fax machine in about 90 seconds. Choose reports from First Call, Standard & Poor's, Argus, Vickers, and Micropal. Reports cost between $1.50 and $4.50 each. Money 101 (created by the editors of *Money* magazine and its Web site) offers electronic lessons that help you invest, save, borrow, and spend more wisely.

SUPPORT SYSTEMS: 1-800-417-7423 for customer support. Standard glossary, financial news and charts, Reuters news summaries. Moving stock ticker across bottom of screen with delayed quotes.

OPERATIONAL SYSTEMS: Standard.

BACKGROUND INFORMATION: National Discount Brokers, Inc. is a publicly traded company listed on the NYSE.

NET.B@NK

URL: www.netbank.com

TYPE OF SITE: Online banking offering online investment services as an account feature.

USERS: All levels of online investors.

SNAIL MAIL: 950 N. Point Parkway, Suite 350
Alpharetta, GA 30005

PHONE: 1-800-277-7700

SERVICES: Real-time quotes. Symbol lookup. Portfolio management report, checkpoint page, dynamic confirmation page. Full brokerage services with free trading assistance.

EXECUTION SYSTEMS: Investments offered through UVEST Investment Services.

FEES:

Account minimum: None. Net.B@nk NetWorth investment account. Automatic dividend reinvestment and daily sweep to money market account. No charge for broker assistance.

Limit/market trades: $25 up to 2000 shares; then add $.015/share for shares over 2000. Add premium of $14 when order is not entered over Internet.

Mutual funds: $25/trade for no-loads. Add premium of $10 when order is not entered over Internet.

Options: $35 + $2.50/contract.

Bonds: $45 + $2/$1000 face value for municipal, zero coupon, corporate, and Treasury bonds.

Treasury bills: $45/trade.

IRA accounts: $35/year.

Margin: Brokers call plus ¾% to 2.75%.

SUPPORT SYSTEMS: Toll-free number and e-mail for customer support. Standard glossary, interactive demo, news headlines, charts, mutual fund spotlight. WallSt.com research reports.

OPERATIONAL SYSTEMS: Standard.

BACKGROUND INFORMATION: Opened in 1996, Net.B@nk, member FDIC, is the nation's largest federal savings bank to operate exclusively through the Internet. Net.B@nk has partnered with UVEST Investment Services, a leading discount brokerage, to offer customers investment products.

THE NET INVESTOR

URL: www.netinvestor.com

TYPE OF SITE: Discount online brokerage.

USERS: All levels of online investors needing little or no assistance.

SNAIL MAIL: 135 S. LaSalle Street, Suite 1500
Chicago, IL 60603

PHONE: 1-800-NET-4250 (638-4250)
1-800-880-4693

E-MAIL: info@netinvestor.com

SERVICES: Portfolio tracking (can include assets held outside Net Investor for comprehensive overview), tax-lot accounting, calendar of key economic news releases. PawTracks to build "hot list" and track unlimited securities at a glance.

EXECUTION SYSTEMS: Proprietary True Price Advantage for price improvement on Nasdaq trades.

FEES:

Account minimum: $5000. Free dividend reinvestment and daily sweep to money market account. $50 annual maintenance fee for inactive accounts. First trade free upon account activation.

Quotes: Unlimited delayed quotes. Real-time quotes available for active traders at $25/month with 1–3 monthly trades; $12.50/month with 4–7 monthly trades; free with 8 or more monthly trades. Otherwise, $50/month.

Limit/market trades: $19.95 + $.01/share for entire order.

Penny stocks: Add $.01/share to standard rates; maximum 4% of principal.

Mutual funds: 4000+ to choose from. No-loads are $35/trade for value up to $15,000; $45/trade for value of $15,000–$100,000; $60/trade for value over $100,000.

Options: $35 + $2.50/contract for contract value of $3 or less; $35 + $3/contract for contract value over $3.

Bonds: $25 + $4/bond, up to 25 bonds. Over 25 bonds, add $3/bond thereafter.

Treasuries: $45/transaction up to $50,000. Add .1% of principal for transactions over $50,000.

IRA accounts: $24/year, $5 setup, $50 closing.

APPEALING FEATURES: Portfolio tracking of assets held outside Net Investor.

SUPPORT SYSTEMS: Toll-free number, e-mail, and message board. Research from Reuters and OnDemand Research, First Call earnings estimates, S&P reports, WallStreet Whispers, Lipper mutual fund reports, Vickers insider trading reports, intraday and historical graphs.

OPERATIONAL SYSTEMS: Standard.

BACKGROUND INFORMATION: The Net Investor is a division of Howe Barnes Investments, Inc., member NYSE, CHX, SIPC, NASD, MSRB, and SIA.

NEWPORT DISCOUNT BROKERAGE, INC.

URL: www.newport-discount.com

TYPE OF SITE: Discount brokerage offering online, touch-tone, or broker-assisted trading. Web TV compatible.

USERS: All levels of online investors. Foreign accounts accepted.

SNAIL MAIL: 5499 N. Federal Highway, Suite N
Boca Raton, FL 33487

PHONE: 1-800-999-FAST (3278)

E-MAIL: newport@newport-discount.com

SERVICES: Portfolio tracking, checkpoint page, confirmation page.

EXECUTION SYSTEMS: Clearing company is U.S. Clearing, a division of Fleet Securities, Inc.

FEES:
  Account minimum: None. No postage/handling charges.
  Quotes: Unlimited delayed quotes. $29.95/month for real-time quotes; free with touch-tone trading.
  Limit/market trades: $19 for any online trade.
  Touch-tone: Add $10.
  Broker-assisted: $30/trade up to 100 shares; $35/trade for 101–300 shares; $40/trade for 301–800 shares; $45/trade for 801–900 shares; $50/trade for 901–1000 shares; plus $1 per 100 shares thereafter up to $60 for 2000 shares.
  Mutual funds: 2000+ to choose from.
  Options: $3–$5/contract; $40 minimum.
  Treasuries: $3/bond up to 49 bonds; $2/bond for 50 or more bonds; $40 minimum. Free dividend reinvestment.
  IRA accounts: No annual or setup fees; $50 closing.

SUPPORT SYSTEMS: Toll-free number and e-mail for customer support. Standard glossary, demo, contextual help feature. Research includes Reuters news and profiles, intraday graphs, Java charts, IPO info, market snapshot, equity indices.

OPERATIONAL SYSTEMS: Standard.

BACKGROUND INFORMATION: Newport Discount Brokerage, Inc., member NASD/SIPC, was established in 1975.

OLDE DISCOUNT CORPORATION

URL: www.oldediscount.com

TYPE OF SITE: Full service brokerage firm providing online trading convenience for clients.

USERS: Clients and retail traders.

SNAIL MAIL: 751 Griswold Street
        Detroit, MI 48226

PHONE: 1-313-961-6666

E-MAIL: Site-directed e-mail for further information on each section.

SERVICES: Client Access section for account holders. Commission, retirement, and tax accounting calculators. Assistance available through many branch offices (nearest branch locator on site). Promotes a variety of money market accounts.

EXECUTION SYSTEMS: Order routing system has direct electronic access to all major U.S. stock exchanges. Sells order flow.

FEES: SmartTrade account allows sophisticated investors with a minimum account equity of $500,000 in any combination of cash or securities to transact 1000 shares or more of a common stock, valued at $5 or more per share, *free* of markups, markdowns, or commission fees. All common stocks listed on the NYSE, AMEX, or Nasdaq qualify. A $1.75 postage/handling fee is added to each transaction. An SEC fee of $\frac{1}{300}$ of 1% of principal value is added to each closing transaction.

For other traders, fees begin at $20 and are quantity-based.

SUPPORT SYSTEMS: Branch offices to support traders.

OPERATIONAL SYSTEMS: Standard plus frames-capable browser and 800×600 dpi resolution.

BACKGROUND INFORMATION: OLDE Discount Corporation is a member of NYSE.

PEREMEL & COMPANY INC.

URL: www.peremel.com

TYPE OF SITE: Full service brokerage offering online, touch-tone, operator, or full broker-assisted trading.

USERS: All levels of online investors.

SNAIL MAIL: Woodholme Business Center
1829 Reisterstown Road, Suite 120
Baltimore, MD 21208

PHONE: 1-800-PEREMEL (737-3635)

E-MAIL: info@peremel.com

SERVICES: Fee-based, portfolio management services available for $100,000 accounts. Financial planning on hourly basis. Wrap portfolio with $100,000 minimum account and quarterly fee.

EXECUTION SYSTEMS: Clearing agent is National Financial Services, Inc.

FEES:

Account minimum: $2000. VIP account requires $15,000.

Market trades: $18 up to 2000 shares; then add $.01/share for entire order.

Limit trades: $20 up to 2000 shares; then add $.01/share for entire order.

Touch-tone: $34/trade (limit or market) up to 2000 shares; then add $.02/share on entire order.

Operator-assisted: $38/trade (limit or market) up to 2000 shares; then add $.02/share on entire order.

Personal broker: $38/trade (limit or market) up to 100 shares; $40/trade for 101–200 shares; $42/trade for 201–300 shares; over 300 shares, $35 + $.03/share.

Penny stocks: $.035/share up to 19,999 shares; $.025/share for 20,000 and over; minimum $38.

Mutual funds: Internet—$25 for no-load funds, $15 for switch. Touch-tone or operator—$35 for no-load funds, $20 for switch. Personal broker—$35 for no-loads valued up to $49,999, $50 for value of $50,000–$99,999, and $75 for value of $100,000 and over; $12.50 for switch.

Options: Overriding minimum of $35 ($38 for broker). Internet—$25 + $1.50/contract under $4 value; or + $2/contract at $4 value and over. Touch-tone or operator—$35 + $2/contract under $4 value or + $2.50/contract at $4 value and over. Personal broker—$3.75/contract under $1 value; for options valued over $1, $6.50/contract up to 10 contracts, $6/contract for 11–20, contracts, $5.50/contract for 21–49, and $4.75/contract for 50 and over.

Bonds: Corporate—$3/bond; $4/bond for personal broker. $35 minimum commission. Operator or broker assistance required.

Treasuries: $50, any size. Operator or broker assistance required.

Margin: Brokers call plus .5% to 2%.

APPEALING FEATURES: IPO investments.

SUPPORT SYSTEMS: Toll-free number and e-mail.

OPERATIONAL SYSTEMS: Standard.

BACKGROUND INFORMATION: Peremel & Company Inc., member NASD/SIPC, was founded in 1974.

PREFERRED TRADE

URL: www.preferredtrade.com

TYPE OF SITE: Discount online brokerage. Not compatible with MacIntosh or Linux operating systems.

USERS: Geared toward self-directed, active traders.

SNAIL MAIL: 220 Montgomery Street, Suite 777
                San Francisco, CA 94104

PHONE: 1-888-889-9178

SERVICES: Real-time snap quote on order entry. Real-time account access, order status, dynamic updating of portfolio and trade history. Real-time confirmations.

EXECUTION SYSTEMS: Trades through Windows-based software with "nonbrowser" Internet delivery. Algorithm automatically selects the routing for order. Traders can override and route orders to ECN or market maker for the $15 (and up) rate, or accept the $7.75 rate available from selling order flow. All transactions are processed through Preferred Capital Markets Inc.

FEES:

Account minimum: $1000. $5000 for margin account. Telephone and broker-assisted orders same as online rates.

Trades: Listed (limit)—$.03/share ($15 minimum); 100–500 shares $15; 1000 shares $30; 5000 shares $150. Includes ECN charges. Nasdaq (market)—$.02/share ($15 minimum); 100–500 shares $15; 1000 shares $20; 5000 shares $100. Includes ECN charges. OTC (limit/market)—With payment for order flow, $7.75/trade, or $.02/share with a $15 minimum for orders routed via Island, SelectNet, and other ECNs. Includes ECN charges.

Options: $2–$3 per contract; $19.95 minimum. Direct access to electronic exchanges via RAES (CBOE), POETS (Pac Exchange), AMOS (AMEX) and AUTOM (Phila Exchange).

Mutual funds: 600+ funds to choose from; fee range $15–$30.

IRA accounts: $45/year; setup $25; $100 closing.

Margin: 7½%.

APPEALING FEATURES: Doesn't use browser; is installed via a disk.

SUPPORT SYSTEMS: Toll-free number. Extensive glossary. Company, industry, and market charts and news available.

OPERATIONAL SYSTEMS: Standard upgrade. Not available for MacIntosh.

BACKGROUND INFORMATION: Preferred Trade is a division of Preferred Capital Markets, Inc.

QUICK & REILLY INC.

URL: www.quickwaynet.com

TYPE OF SITE: Full service brokerage offering discounted online trading.

USERS: All levels of online traders. Foreign accounts accepted.

SNAIL MAIL: 26 Broadway, 11th Floor
New York, NY 10004

PHONE: 1-800-453-2517

SERVICES: Free portfolio tracker.

EXECUTION SYSTEMS: Clearing company is U.S. Clearing Corp.

FEES:

Account minimum: None. $2000 for margin account.

Quotes: 100 real-time quotes upon account activation, plus 100 with each trade.

Market trades: $14.95/trade up to 5000 shares; then add $.02/share for all shares over 5000.

Limit trades: $19.95/trade up to 5000 shares; then add $.02/share for all shares over 5000.

Broker-assisted: Minimum overriding fee of $37.50. Minimum charge is $.06/share of first 1000 shares, plus $.03/share thereafter. Maximum charge is $49 for first 100 shares, plus $.50/share thereafter.

$22 + .014% of principal for trades up to $2500

$38 + .0045% of principal for trades of $2501–$6000

$59 + .0025% of principal for trades of $6001–$22,000

$77 + .0017% of principal for trades of $22,001–$50,000

$120 + .00085% of principal for trades of $50,001–$500,000

$205 + .00068% of principal for trades over $500,000

Options: 10% off regular fees. Minimum is $37.50 + $1.75/contract. Maximum is $40 for each of first two contracts, plus $4 for each additional contract.

$29 + .016% of principal for trades up to $2500

$49 + .008% of principal for trades of $2501–$10,000

$99 + .003% of principal for trades over $10,000

IRA accounts: Free with $10,000 account; otherwise, $25/year. Free setup.

Mutual funds: 2500+ to choose from, with 295 available at no transaction fee. Fees up to $25.

Penny stocks: Same rates as online stocks. Broker-assisted rates are $37 + 3% of principal.

Canadian/foreign stocks: Available at broker-assisted rates.

Bonds: Corporate—$4 per $1000 face value or 1% of principal, whichever is less. Overriding minimum of $37.50.

Treasuries: $50/transaction.

Margin: Brokers call plus .75% to 2%.

SUPPORT SYSTEMS: 24-hour customer support via 1-800-7220 and e-mail. Extensive FAQs and glossary. Research/news includes Baseline, Zacks, InvesTools, MarketEdge SecondOpinion, Big Charts, Java charts, Briefing.com, Inc. link, Market Movers, Reuters, and Reuters News.

OPERATIONAL SYSTEMS: Standard.

BACKGROUND INFORMATION: Quick & Reilly Inc. is a wholly-owned subsidiary of Fleet Bank.

CHARLES SCHWAB & CO. INC.

URL: www.schwab.com

TYPE OF SITE: Full service brokerage offering discounted online services to clients.

USERS: All levels of online investors and institutions.

SNAIL MAIL: 101 Montgomery Street
San Francisco, CA 94104

PHONE: 1-800-435-4000

E-MAIL: Site directed.

SERVICES: Portfolio management includes asset allocation tool kit, confirmation page with online and mail acknowledgment, checkpoint page for review and to confirm or cancel orders.

FEES:

Account minimum:

Schwab Account: $2500 minimum; $29 annual maintenance fee. Fee waived if account balance is above $10,000 on September 15 of each year (or if you invest $100/month in MoneyLink® or make 2 or more commissionable trades in preceding 12 months).

SchwabOne Account: $10,000 minimum; $15/quarter maintenance fee. Fee waived if account balance is over $10,000 during the last 5 business days of each quarter (or if you invest $100/month in MoneyLink® or make 2 or more commissionable trades in preceding 12 months). Includes BillPay™.

Advisor Source: $100,000 account minimum for fee-based advisory services. Call 1-888-774-3756 to enroll.

Schwab Signature Account: Includes Access Online checking and no maintenance fee. Call 1-800-450-0669 to enroll.

Schwab Signature Service™—$100,000 minimum or $10,000 + 12 annual trades

Schwab Signature Gold™—$500,000 minimum or $25,000 + 24 annual trades

Schwab Signature Platinum™—$1,000,000 minimum or $50,000 + 48 annual trades

Quotes: Real-time quotes available by touch-tone; delayed quotes on Web.

Trades: $29.95 for up to 1000 shares or $.03/share for Web trades over 1000 shares. 20% discount off standard broker-assisted commissions/transaction fees for Web trades for mutual funds, $35 minimum commission for Treasuries, corporate bonds, and options. No-fee StockBuilder Plan® for free dividend reinvestment when specified at time of trade for qualifying stocks.

Touch-tone: (1-800-272-4922) 10% discount off stated broker-assisted commissions/transaction fees.

APPEALING FEATURES: Multiple levels of service and support.

SUPPORT SYSTEMS: Toll-free numbers and e-mail. Site map and glossary. Research/news includes market data with performance snapshot, multiple quotes, charts, corporate reports, EDGAR link.

OPERATIONAL SYSTEMS: Standard.

BACKGROUND INFORMATION: Charles Schwab & Co. Inc. is a member of SIPC and NYSE.

SCOTTSDALE SECURITIES, INC.—SCOT TRADE

URL: www.scottrade.com

TYPE OF SITE: Full service brokerage offering discounted online trading.

USERS: All levels of online traders. U.S. residents only. No mutual funds, penny stocks, Canadian stocks, or foreign stocks online.

SNAIL MAIL: P.O. Box 31759
                              St. Louis, MO 63131

PHONE: 1-800-619-SAVE (619-7283)

SERVICES: 90 offices throughout the U.S. for full brokerage services.

FEES:

Account minimum: $2000. Requires 75% of account trades to be ordered online.

Quotes: 100 free real-time quotes per trade. Level I quotes via North American Quotation for $32/month.

Market trades: $7 for any size trade.

Limit trades: $12 for any size trade.

Touch-tone: $5 extra; 12 minutes free with each trade. Otherwise, $.10/minute.

Broker-assisted: $10 extra.

Options: $20 + $1.60/contract; assignments $17. Broker-assisted rates are: $27.50 + .004% of principal + $1.25/contract; minimum $32.

IRA accounts: No annual or setup fee; $60 closing.

Margin: Brokers call plus .5%.

SUPPORT SYSTEMS: Toll-free number. Site demo.

OPERATIONAL SYSTEMS: Standard.

BACKGROUND INFORMATION: Scottsdale Securities, Inc. member NASD/SIPC, began offering discounted commissions in 1980.

SURETRADE, INC.

URL: www.suretrade.com

TYPE OF SITE: Deep discount brokerage. No Canadian or foreign stocks.

USERS: Online traders needing little assistance; foreign accounts accepted.

SNAIL MAIL: P.O. Box 862
Lincoln, RI 02865-0862

PHONE: 1-401-642-6900

SERVICES: Touch-tone trading, Options desk, Margin desk, Funds center. Portfolio management report, confirmation page, trade executions noted by day.

EXECUTION SYSTEMS: U.S. Clearing Corp.

FEES:

Account minimum: None; $2000 for margin.
Quotes: 100 free real-time quotes per day.
Trades: For stocks valued at $2+/share.
Limit: $9.95 up to 5000 shares; then add .01/share for entire order.
Market: $7.95 up to 5000 shares; then add .01/share for entire order.
Touch-tone: Add $4 extra per trade. (MarketTouch system 1-800-362-6275.)
Broker assisted: Add $25 extra per trade.
Penny/BB stocks: valued at less than $2/share: $5 extra for the first 5000 shares, then add .01/share for entire order.
Options: $20 + $1.70/contract ($28.95 minimum).
Mutual funds: $25/trade for no-loads.
Margin rate: Brokers call less .5% to less 1%.

APPEALING FEATURES: Easy access pull-down menu to extensive free research.

SUPPORT SYSTEMS: Online application. 800 number issued to account holders; screen view demo; standard glossary; Baseline, BigCharts, Briefing.com, InvesTools, MarketEdge, iSyndicate, Reuters, and Zacks.

OPERATIONAL SYSTEMS: Standard.

BACKGROUND INFORMATION: SURETRADE was launched in November 1997 as part of the Quick & Reilly Group, which was later acquired by Fleet Financial Group.

TRADE-WELL DISCOUNT INVESTING, LLC

URL: www.trade-well.com

TYPE OF SITE: Discount online brokerage, including foreign equities.

USERS: All levels of online investors.

SNAIL MAIL: 25 Broadway, 7th Floor
New York, NY 10004-1010

PHONE: 1-888-907-9797

SERVICES: Also offers trading through PC, wireless, touch-tone phone, or broker. Trade-Well portfolio provides account details, balances, positions, history, and order status. Balance page has account value, current as of close of previous business day. Position page charts account in pie graph. Checkpoint page allows review and verification/cancellation of open orders and confirmation through order-tracking number. Free real-time quotes.

EXECUTION SYSTEMS: Clearing firm is BHC Securities, Inc.

FEES:

Account minimum: None. $5000 for margin accounts. All trades subject to $3.50 postage/handling charge.

Quotes: Real-time quotes available through Polaris software for $75/month or free after 25 trades/month.

Limit/market trades: $22/trade up to 3000 shares; then add $.01/share on entire order.

Broker-assisted: $27 per trade up to 3000 shares; then add $.01/share on entire order.

Options: $21 + $1.50/contract if option price is less than $1; + $2 for value between $1 and $3⅞; + $2.50 for value between $4 and $7⅞; + $3.50 for value of $8 and over.

Mutual funds: $27 fee for no-load funds. Free dividend reinvestment.

Bonds: Corporate—$27 + $3/bond for 1–50 bonds; + $2/bond for 50+ bonds. Munis, zeros, Treasuries, UITs—$50/transaction.

IRA accounts: Free.

Margin: Brokers call plus ½% to 2%.

SUPPORT SYSTEMS: Toll-free number and e-mail. Glossary, integrated help feature, calculator. Research/news includes Baseline and WallStreet on Demand. Bridge Financial Information available on Polaris software (see Quote pricing).

OPERATIONAL SYSTEMS: Standard.

BACKGROUND INFORMATION: Trade-Well Discount is an affiliate of Josephthal & Co. Inc., an investment banking company established in 1910. Member NASD/SIPC.

TRU TRADE

URL: www.trutrade.com

TYPE OF SITE: Discount online brokerage.

USERS: All levels of online traders. Foreign accounts accepted. Check for registration in your state. Not available in AL, AK, HI, ID, ME, MS, OK, OR, RI, VT, WA, or WY.

SNAIL MAIL: 142 Northstar West
619 Marquette Ave. S
Minneapolis, MN 55402-1701

PHONE: Levitt & Levitt Discount 1-800-671-8505
ReCom Securities 1-800-328-8600

E-MAIL: info@levitt-levitt.com

SERVICES: Real-time quotes. Portfolio tracker through Reality Online, a Reuters company.

EXECUTION SYSTEMS: Clearing firm is U.S. Clearing Corp., a division of Fleet Securities, Inc.

FEES:
Account minimum: $5000.
Limit/market trades: Listed—$12.95/trade up to 1999 shares; then add $.01/share on entire order. OTC—$12.95/trade up to 1999 shares; then free for stocks priced at $5+.
Broker-assisted: $35/trade and up.
Mutual funds: $25/trade for some no-loads; 1500+ funds to choose from.
Options: $2–$4/contract; $29 minimum.
IRA accounts: Free; free setup; $50 closing.

SUPPORT SYSTEMS: Toll-free numbers. Static demo page. FAQs.

OPERATIONAL SYSTEMS: Standard.

BACKGROUND INFORMATION: Tru Trade is offered through the Levitt & Levitt Deep Discount Brokerage Division of ReCom Securities Inc., founded in 1977, member NASD/SIPC.

U.S. RICA FINANCIAL

URL: www.usrica.com

TYPE OF SITE: Online brokerage.

USERS: All levels of online traders.

SNAIL MAIL: 1630 Oakland Road, Suite A208
            San Jose, CA 85131

PHONE: 1-888-887-7422

E-MAIL: customerservice@usrica.com

SERVICES: Standard Reality Online package. Real-time quotes require outside vendor. Free delayed quotes. Offers IPOs.

EXECUTION SYSTEMS: Clearing agent is U.S. Clearing.

FEES:
>   *Account minimum:* $2000. First trade free with $10,000 account activation. Add $2.50 postage/handling fee to each trade.
>   *Limit/market trades:* $10/trade for 1 to 499 shares. $4.95/trade over 500 shares.
>   *Touch-tone:* $15/trade. $5 discount for trades over 500 shares.
>   *Broker-assisted:* $35/trade.
>   *Penny stock:* $.02/share; $35 minimum; $100 maximum.

APPEALING FEATURES: Site search button.

SUPPORT SYSTEMS: Toll-free number. Demo, chat room, and glossary.

OPERATIONAL SYSTEMS: Standard.

BACKGROUND INFORMATION: US Rica Financial Inc., member NASD/SIPC, was founded in 1995.

VANGUARD BROKERAGES SERVICES— ACCESS VBS

URL: www.vanguard.com

TYPE OF SITE: Online trading facility for the Vanguard Group, specializing in mutual funds.

USERS: All levels of online investors.

SNAIL MAIL: Access VBS Online Trading
              100 Vanguard Boulevard
              Malvern, PA 19355

PHONE: 1-800-992-8327

E-MAIL: Site-directed.

SERVICES: Stock, mutual fund, and options trading. Account information, including balances, holdings, history, and order status. Real-time and delayed quotes, with quick quotes and symbol/company lookup. Secure messaging with VBS Associates. Tracking and research tools.

EXECUTION SYSTEMS: Clearing agent is the Pershing™ Division of Donaldson, Lufkin & Jenrette Securities.

FEES:

   Account assistance: 1-800-285-4563.

   Quotes: 250 real-time quotes on account activation; 100 additional with each executed trade.

   Limit/market trades: For stocks priced less than $1, a fee of $30 + 3% of principal will apply. Internet—$20 or $.02/share, whichever is greater. AutoBroker—$40 or $.02/share, whichever is greater. Order desk—$45 or $.03/share, whichever is greater.

   Options: Internet—$30 + $1.50/contract. AutoBroker—$30 + $2/contract. Order desk—$30 + $2.50/contract.

   Mutual funds: FundAccess—Over 2000 funds (use site's FundSearch) at $35/transaction (non-Vanguard funds).

   Bonds: Corporate—$25 + $2/bond ($35 minimum). Treasury—$50/transaction; at auction, $25/transaction.

APPEALING FEATURES: Availability of Vanguard funds online.

SUPPORT SYSTEMS: Toll-free number. Learning Center and Planning Center. Extensive research and news; portfolio tools.

Download forms to open account.

OPERATIONAL SYSTEMS: Standard.

BACKGROUND INFORMATION: Vanguard Brokerages Services is part of the Vanguard Group Inc., founded in 1974. Access VBS is their low-cost provider of online trading.

VISION TRADE

URL: www.visiontrade.com

TYPE OF SITE: Discount online brokerage. No penny stocks.

USERS: All levels of online traders, with emphasis on active traders. Available only to residents of CA, CT, DE, FL, GA, KS, MA, MD, ME, NH, NJ, NY, OH, OK, OR, PA, RI, VA, VT, and WA.

SNAIL MAIL: 310 Central Avenue
 Lawrence, NY 11559

PHONE: 1-800-374-1940

SERVICES: Delayed quotes and price history. Deeper discount based on trading frequency. Symbol lookup.

EXECUTION SYSTEMS: Clearing company is U.S. Clearing Corp.

FEES:

Account minimum: None. Trade discounts are retroactive to first trade of month. Active traders will be refunded commission discount at month's end.

Quotes: Real-time quotes at $30/month.

Limit/market trades: 1–50 trades per month, $16/trade; 51–99 trades per month, $12.95/trade; 100+ trades per month, $10.95/trade. Equity trades over 5000 shares, add $.01/share for entire order.

Broker-assisted: Add $20/trade.

Mutual funds: $25/transaction for certain no-load funds.

Options: $20 + $1.50/contract with a $25 minimum for options under $1; $20 + $2/contract with a $25 minimum for options at $1 and over.

IRA accounts: No annual or setup fees; $50 closing.

Margin: Brokers call less .5% to 1%.

SUPPORT SYSTEMS: Long-distance number (1-516-374-2184) and e-mail. Demo and standard glossary. Research includes link to Market Snapshot Inc., Java charts, intraday graphs, currency rates, hot stock list, economic calendar, and Zacks research.

OPERATIONAL SYSTEMS: Standard.

BACKGROUND INFORMATION: Vision Trade is a division of Vision Securities, Inc.

WALL STREET DISCOUNT CORPORATION

URL: www.wsdc.com

TYPE OF SITE: Discount broker offering U.S. and foreign security trades by touch-tone, online, and broker.

USERS: All levels of online traders.

SNAIL MAIL: 100 Wall Street
New York, NY 10005

PHONE: 1-888-44-WALLST (449-2557)

E-MAIL: info@wsdc.com

EXECUTION SYSTEMS: Clearing firm is Ernst & Company. (May sell order flow.)

FEES:

Account minimum: None.

Quotes: 100 free real-time quotes on account activation; 100 additional with each executed trade.

Limit/market trades: Internet—$19.95. Phone—$24.95. Broker—$29.95. Rates apply to first 2500 shares. Add $.015/share for additional shares over 2500.

Options: $29.95 minimum; graduated commission per contract ($1.50 to $5.25) based on option prices (from $\frac{1}{16}$ to 20+).

Mutual funds: 400+ to choose from at $30–$100/trade, based on transaction amounts of $1000 to $100,000+. Automatic dividend reinvestment.

Bonds: Corporate—$29.95 minimum; $2.50/bond.

Margin: Brokers call less $\frac{1}{4}$% (subject to change).

SUPPORT SYSTEMS: Toll-free number and e-mail. Glossary. Standard portfolio management reports. Free charts, news, and research.

OPERATIONAL SYSTEMS: Standard.

BACKGROUND INFORMATION: The Wall Street Discount Corporation, member NYSE, NASD, MSRB, and SIPC, was founded in 1978.

WALL ST ELECTRONICA ONLINE TRADING, INC.

URL: www.wallstreete.com

TYPE OF SITE: Discount online brokerage.

USERS: Online traders—individuals, professionals, and institutions.

SNAIL MAIL: 7242 SW 42nd Street
            Miami, FL 33135

PHONE: 1-888-WALL-ST E (925-5783)

E-MAIL: info@wallstreete.com

SERVICES: Real-time quotes. Customized portfolio manager.

EXECUTION SYSTEMS: Clearing company is Herzog Heine Geduld Inc.

FEES:

Account minimum: None. Automatic daily sweep into one of 4 money market funds.

Quotes: Free real-time quotes (limit: 100 per day) on opening an account.

Trades: OTC limit/market—$14.95/trade + $.02/share above 1000 shares. Listed, limit/stop, GTC—$19.95/trade + $.02/share.

Broker-assisted: Add $20 + $.01/share.

Options: $25 + $2.50/contract. Exercise or assignment $25.

Bonds: $35 minimum; $5/unit of $1000.

IRA accounts: Free setup; $25 annual fee; $50 closing.

Margin: Approximately 1.25% over broker's call.

SUPPORT SYSTEMS: Toll-free number and e-mail. Contextual page help in demo. Customized trading and analytical tools, options tutorial, margin FAQs.

OPERATIONAL SYSTEMS: Standard.

BACKGROUND INFORMATION: WallStreet Electronica Online Trading, Inc. is a member of NASD/SIPC.

WANG INVESTMENT ASSOCIATES, INC.

URL: www.wangvest.com

TYPE OF SITE: Full service brokerage offering deep discounted online trading.

USERS: All levels of online traders, including foreign accounts.

SNAIL MAIL: 41-60 Main Street, Suite 209
Flushing, NY 11355

PHONE: 1-800-353-9264
1-718-353-9264 (international)

E-MAIL: info@wangvest.com

SERVICES: Stocks (listed, OTC, foreign, and ADRs), options, equity and index U.S. Treasury securities, municipal bonds, corporate bonds, CDs, UITs, agency securities (FNMA, GNMA, etc.), zero coupons, bonds, mutual funds. Obtain real-time quotes and/or review account activities 24 hours, 7 days a week.

EXECUTION SYSTEMS: Clearing agent is National Financial Services, Inc.

FEES:

Account minimum: $15,000. Daily money market sweep with interest credited monthly. All odd-lot trades subject to a minimum $15 commission fee.

Quotes: Unlimited delayed quotes. $10/month for real-time quotes or subscribe to Market Data through DTN.IQ for $79/month with $50 initiation fee plus exchange fees.

Trades: $5/trade on all NYSE, AMEX, and Nasdaq market orders for 1000 shares or more of a stock valued at $5 or more. $8/trade on all NYSE, AMEX, and Nasdaq limit orders and market orders under 1000 shares.

Touch-tone: 1-800-298-0585. $15/trade on all NYSE, AMEX, and Nasdaq market/limit orders for any number of shares at any price.

Broker-assisted: U.S. stocks, $22/trade. Options, $20/trade + $2/contract; $30 minimum.

Mutual funds: $25 flat fee for no-loads regardless of investment size.

IRA accounts: Maintenance fees waived if account equity is $10,000 or greater.

Options: $15/trade + $1.75/contract for any contract price; $25 minimum.

Canadian stocks: $22 + $.02/share.

Foreign stocks: $125 + $.02/share.

Bonds: Listed corporate—$25 + $2/bond. Zero coupon—$50.

Treasury bills: $50.

Margin: Debit balances below $25,000, 2% above brokers call; $25,000–$49,000, 1½% above brokers call; $50,000–$99,000, 1% above brokers call; $100,000 and up, ½% above brokers call.

APPEALING FEATURES: Banking services.

SUPPORT SYSTEMS: Interactive demo. Links to Barron's Online, Bloomberg, Chicago Mercantile Exchange, NYSE, Yahoo! Finance, DBC Online, Nasdaq, Microsoft Investor, Thomson Investors Network, Taiwan Stock Exchange, WSJ.com, Wall Street City, Briefing.com, CheckFree Investment Services, AMEX.

OPERATIONAL SYSTEMS: Adobe Acrobat to download forms.

BACKGROUND INFORMATION: Wang Investment Associates Inc., member NASD/SIPC and MSRB, is a registered broker/dealer established in 1986.

WATERHOUSE SECURITIES

URL: www.waterhouse.com

TYPE OF SITE: Discount brokerage offering online and touch-tone trading.

USERS: All levels of online traders and fee-based advisors. Foreign accounts accepted.

SNAIL MAIL: 48 Water Street
New York, NY 10275-0205

PHONE: 1-800-934-4410

E-MAIL: Online icon.

SERVICES: Account provides upgraded reporting features. Waterhouse DirectDownload works with Quicken 98, Quicken 99, Quicken.com, and Microsoft Money 98, Money 99, and MSN to deliver financial information electronically from Waterhouse Securities directly into personal finance software. 160 branch offices nationwide.

EXECUTION SYSTEMS: Clearing firm is National Investors Services Corp.

FEES:

Account minimum: $1000 for a webBroker account.

Quotes: 100 free real-time quotes on opening account; additional 100 per trade. Otherwise, $5/100 quotes.

Limit/market trades: $12 for up to 5000 shares; then $.01/share for entire order.

Touch-tone: $35 for up to 5000 shares; then $.01/share for entire order.

Broker-assisted: $45 for up to 5000 shares; then $.01/share for entire order.

BB and Canadian stocks: Available only through broker.

Options: $45 for assignments. Option chains available from $28.13 to $252.90.

Mutual funds: 7100+ to choose from, including 1000 with no fee. $24/transaction when applicable.

Bonds: $2.50/$1000 bond; $35 minimum.

IRA accounts: Free.

Margin: Brokers call plus ½% to 1%.

APPEALING FEATURES: IPOs plus Index fund and Waterhouse Dow 30 Fund. Earn American Airlines mileage with TD Waterhouse account.

SUPPORT SYSTEMS: Toll-free number and e-mail. Research includes Stock Screening by Market Guide, Briefing.com, S&P reports, Zacks estimates.

OPERATIONAL SYSTEMS: Standard.

BACKGROUND INFORMATION: Waterhouse Securities, Inc., member NYSE and SIPC, and Waterhouse National Bank are both wholly-owned subsidiaries of Waterhouse Investor Services, Inc., which recently merged with Kennedy Cabot.

WELLS FARGO BANK—WELLS TRADE

URL: www.wellsfargo.com/wellstrade/

TYPE OF SITE: Full service brokerage subsidiary of bank, offering on-line trading convenience.

USERS: All levels of online traders. Foreign accounts accepted.

SNAIL MAIL: 5599 San Felipe, Suite 1400
Houston, TX 77056

PHONE: 1-800-TRADERS (872-3377)

SERVICES: Symbol lookup. Account reports include summary screen portfolio, open order screen, online confirmation.

EXECUTION SYSTEMS: Brokerage accounts are carried and cleared through BHC Securities Inc., member NASD/SIPC and NYSE. Securities products are offered through Fiserv Investor Services (FIS). BHC and FIS are affiliates and neither is an affiliate of Wells Fargo Bank or Wells Fargo Securities.

FEES:

Account minimum: $1000.

Quotes: 100 real-time quotes on account activation; 100 additional per trade.

Limit/market trades: $29.95/trade up to 1000 shares of any stock; then add $.03/share for entire order. $34.95/trade up to 1000 shares.

Broker-assisted: $.09/share for first 1000 shares, + $.04/share thereafter for stocks below $5/share, or $.05/share thereafter for stocks $5+/share. Overriding minimum of $34.95/trade. Maximum $55 for first 100 shares + $.55/share thereafter.

Penny stocks: $34 + 4% of principal.

Options: Overriding minimum of $34.95 and maximum of $40/contract for first 2 contracts, + $4/contract thereafter. 20% off these rates for Internet trades; 10% off for touch-tone trades. With premiums of $.50 or less—from $1.80/contract + 1.5% of principal to $.60/contract + 1.5% of principal, for 1500+ contracts. With premiums greater than $.50—from $29 + 1.6% of principal to $99 + .3% of principal, for $10,000+.

Mutual funds: Overriding minimum of $34.95. 20% off these rates for Internet trades; 10% off for touch-tone trades.

Bonds: Available only through broker.

IRA accounts: Free for $10,000 account or 2 trades/year. Otherwise, $24 annual fee with free setup. Closing $30.

APPEALING FEATURES: Integrated banking services.

SUPPORT SYSTEMS: Toll-free number and e-mail. Demo. Research includes Mutual Fund Explorer, News Alert, charts, market summary, headlines, S&P, Zacks.

OPERATIONAL SYSTEMS: Standard.

BACKGROUND INFORMATION: Wells Trade brokerage accounts are available through Wells Fargo Securities, member NASD/SIPC, a subsidiary of Wells Fargo Bank.

JACK WHITE WEBBROKER

URL: www.jackwhiteco.com

TYPE OF SITE: Full service brokerage.

USERS: All levels of online investors. Foreign accounts accepted.

SNAIL MAIL: 9191 Towne Centre Drive
San Diego, CA 92122

PHONE: 1-800-753-1700

SERVICES: Account reports of up to 10 securities in portfolio. Total account history. View open orders and receive online confirmation.

EXECUTION SYSTEMS: Clearing agent is National Investor Securities Corporation. Commodities through ADM Investor Services.

FEES:

Account minimum: $1000.

Quotes: Unlimited delayed quotes. 100 free real-time quotes per account, plus 100 additional free with each trade.

Limit/market trades: $12 for up to 5000 shares of any stock; then add $.01/share for entire order. Orders sent directly to exchanges.

Touch-tone: 10% discount from broker-assisted rates through TelePath.

Broker-assisted: $33 + $.03/share for up to 1999 shares; then $.02/share for entire order.

Penny stocks: Same as broker rates.

Options: $33 + $3/contract through broker only.

IRA accounts: Free for $10,000 account. Otherwise, $35 annual with free setup.

Commodities: $75 round turn for one contract; $55 for 2 contracts; $45 for 3 contracts.

Mutual funds: $27 fee ($24 online); 6700+ to choose from, including 1300 with no fee. Short sales only through broker.

Bonds: Corporate—$33/transaction + $3 per $1000 of principal amount; $50 minimum.

Treasuries: $33 for bonds bought at auction; otherwise, $50 or priced on net basis.

Margin: Brokers call plus ½% to 1%.

SUPPORT SYSTEMS: Toll-free number and e-mail. Symbol lookup. Demo. Research includes Mutual Fund Network Guide with search tools, charts, market summary, headlines, S&P, Zacks, Briefing.com, MarketEdge, Morningstar, and Market Guide.

OPERATIONAL SYSTEMS: Standard.

BACKGROUND INFORMATION: First established in 1973, Jack White Brokerage, Inc. was purchased in June 1998 by Waterhouse Securities (www.waterhouse.com).

WIT CAPITAL

URL: www.witcapital.com

TYPE OF SITE: Full service online brokerage firm.

USERS: All levels of online traders.

SNAIL MAIL: 8826 Broadway, 6th Floor
New York, NY 10003

PHONE: 1-888-2WITCAP (294-8227)

E-MAIL: members@witcapital.com

SERVICES: At the time of printing, Wit was beta testing a new site to include IPO and venture capital investments. Main site still operational. Full portfolio management report, e-mail confirmation. Statements mailed monthly.

EXECUTION SYSTEMS: Clearing firm is U.S. Clearing Corp.

FEES:
Account minimum: $2000.
Trading Desk: 1-888-394-8227.
Quotes: Unlimited delayed quotes. 100 free real-time quotes on opening account; additional 100 for each trade.
Limit trades: Listed—$19.95 up to 5000 shares; then $.01/share for entire order. OTC—$19.95 for any number of shares.
Market trades: Listed—$14.95 up to 5000 shares; then $.01/share for entire order. OTC—$14.95 for any number of shares.
Touch-tone: 1-888-310-6648. $.27/minute connect fee; 12 free minutes with each trade.
Penny stocks: $25 + 2.75% of principal.
Foreign stocks: Canadian—$30 + $.02/share. Other—$125 + $.02/share.
Mutual funds: 3800+ to choose from; $25 for no-loads.
IRA accounts: Free with $10,000 account; otherwise, $25/year.
Options: $27 minimum; $1.75–$3/contract.
Margin: Brokers call plus ¾% to 2½%.

SUPPORT SYSTEMS: 1-888-594-8227 and e-mail for customer support. Standard glossary, screen shot demo. Research includes News Alert, headlines, charts, Zacks, and Mutual Fund Explorer.

OPERATIONAL SYSTEMS: Standard.

BACKGROUND INFORMATION: Wit Capital, member NASD/SIPC, opened for online business in September 1997.

WYSE SECURITIES

URL: www.wyse-sec.com

TYPE OF SITE: Online brokerage firm.

USERS: All levels of online traders. Currently registered in CA, NV, NY, WA, CO, KY, SD, MD, LA, ID, UT, WV, FL, SC, MI, and NJ.

SNAIL MAIL: 20735 Stevens Creek Boulevard, Suite C
Cupertino, CA 95014

PHONE: 1-800-640-8668
1-408-343-2900

E-MAIL: johnh@hooked.net

SERVICES: Portfolio Tracker lets you track 10 portfolios, each with up to 30 quotes, both online and via e-mail.

EXECUTION SYSTEMS: Clearing company is U.S. Clearing, a division of Fleet Securities, Inc.

FEES:

Account minimum: $2000. $4.50 postage/handling fee applies to all trades.

Quotes: Unlimited real-time quotes for $29.95/month.

Trades: $7.95 flat commission on all Internet stock trades (OTC and listed, market or limit). Round lot share price $1 and up.

Penny stocks: $25 + 2.75% of principal amount.

Broker-assisted: 19.95 flat. Round lot share price over $1.

Bonds: $4/bond.

Mutual Funds: $34/transaction.

GTC (Good Till Cancelled) orders: add $3/order.

Options: Cleared funds must be in account before option orders are placed. Principal amount $0–$2500, $17 + 1.7% of principal; $2501–$10,000, $36 + 0.8% of principal; $10,000 and up, $59 + 0.03% of principal.

IRA accounts: No minimum; no maintenance or setup fees.

Margin: Debit balances $25,000 and above, $\frac{3}{4}$% above brokers call; $20,000–$24,999, 1% above brokers call; $15,000 to $19,999, $1\frac{1}{4}$% above brokers call; $10,000–$14,999, $1\frac{1}{2}$% above brokers call; $5000 to $9999, 1¾% above brokers call; below $5000, 2% above brokers call.

SUPPORT SYSTEMS: Interactive demo. Standard glossary. Zacks research, IPO info, digiTRADE, Second Opinion.

OPERATIONAL SYSTEMS: Standard.

BACKGROUND INFORMATION: Wyse Securities, Member SIPC, MSRB, PCX, and CHX, is a division of Pyramid Financial Corporation, which was incorporated in 1989.

ZIEGLER THRIFT TRADING, INC.

URL: www.ziegler-thrift.com

TYPE OF SITE: Discount brokerage offering online, touch-tone, and PC trading.

USERS: All levels of online investors; includes all U.S. and Canadian markets.

SNAIL MAIL: 733 Marquette Avenue, Suite 106
                  Minneapolis, MN 55402

PHONE: 1-800-3228-4854

E-MAIL: ziegler@primenet.com

SERVICES: Complete portfolio, confirmation (checkpoint) page, daily activity page, 6 branch offices.

EXECUTION SYSTEMS: Clearing firm is U.S. Clearing, a division of Fleet Securities, Inc.

FEES:
> *Account minimum:* None.
> *Quotes:* Free delayed quotes, plus real-time quotes for $29.95/month.
> *Limit/market trades:* InvestRoute (internet)—Minimum $19.73 for up to 1973 shares; $.01/share thereafter.
> *Touch-tone and PC:* MarketTouch 25% off broker-assisted rates.
> *Broker-assisted:* ZTT Account—value-based; $15 + 1% of principal for 100 shares and up, based on value; $34 minimum.
> *Penny stocks:* $25 + 4% of principal.
> *Options:* $27 + $1.50/contract and up, based on value.
> *IRA account:* $40 annual fee; $25 setup; $60 closing.
> *Bonds:* Corporate—$37 + $3/bond.
> *Treasuries:* $40/transaction.

SUPPORT SYSTEMS: Toll-free number and e-mail. Glossary. Interactive demo. Research/news includes free charts, news and research, Inc. link, Zacks, Red Herring, Moneyclub.

OPERATIONAL SYSTEMS: Standard.

BACKGROUND INFORMATION: In August 1999, Ziegler Thrift Trading, Inc., entered into an agreement to be purchased by Strong Capital Management, Inc., of Milwaukee, WI. The Ziegler Companies established ZIT in 1973 as a wholly-owned subsidiary, along with BC Ziegler and Company, an investment banking firm since 1902.

Level II
Trading Sites

The following sites provide more comprehensive quote data generally sought by active, or short-term, traders.

CASTLE ONLINE

URL: www.castleonline.com

TYPE OF SITE: Full service brokerage firm offering Level II trading online. No options, mutual funds, or BB stocks online at this time. Penny stocks through JavaTrader only.

USERS: Active online traders. Check for registration in your state.

SNAIL MAIL: 45 Church Street
              Freeport, NY 11520

PHONE: 1-516-868-8812

E-MAIL: paul@castleonline.com

SERVICES: Free real-time quotes. Free proprietary software, MyTrack Basic, includes intraday and other charts, stock watch, time of sales, and portfolio manager.

EXECUTION SYSTEMS: Trading through Killkey and JavaTrader. A $1/transaction miscellaneous handling fee is charged by clearing agent J.B. Oxford & Company.

FEES:

Account minimum: $5000.

Data fees: Two Level II quote account options (similar to RealTick III) are available. Prince—$150/month or free with 100/trades per month. King—AT Financial Major Attitude data package for $300/month or $150/month with 100 trades per month; free with 150 trades per month. Limited offer of first 5 trades free with Prince or King account.

Limit/market trades: Listed—$19.95 + $.01/share. Nasdaq—$19.95 up to 10,000 shares. (Add $1 for partial execution.) Plus $1 handling fee from clearing agent for each trade.

Broker-assisted: Accounts available through Castle Securities Corp.

ECN fees: $.015/share for any ECN other than Island.

Margin: Brokers call, currently 6½% (subject to change with J.B. Oxford).

APPEALING FEATURES: Software help pages and slide show.

SUPPORT SYSTEMS: Toll-free support via 1-800-661-5133 or 1-800-891-1003 (8:30 am–5 pm EST) and e-mail. Online chat room; TEACH-DAQ training link.

OPERATIONAL SYSTEMS: Standard upgrade.

BACKGROUND INFORMATION: Castle Online, a division of Castle Securities Corp., began operations as a securities broker in 1985 and is a member of NASD/SIPC.

DAYLIGHT TRADING

URL: www.daylighttrading.com

TYPE OF SITE: A professional day trading firm that acts as an agency only. Provides online, electronic, and SOES trading.

USERS: Active day traders. Check for registration in your state.

SNAIL MAIL: 11200 N. Howard Street
                Glendale, CA 91207

PHONE: 1-800-818-0048

E-MAIL: info@daylighttrading.com, tradebuddy@hotmail.com

SERVICES: Data Entitlement software includes RealTick III order entry, Nasdaq Level II quotes, time of sales, technical studies, market minders, and other features. Daily short list.

EXECUTION SYSTEMS: No payment accepted for order flow; all trades executed on an agency basis. Clearing firm is Penson Financial Services.

FEES:

Account minimum: $10,000 and an average of 2 trades per day.

Data fees: $255/month for Data Entitlement. IP-based trading platform delivers real-time streaming market data and live executions. Free with over 150 trades per month. Otherwise, $30/month for NYSE; $35/month for AMEX; $15/month for CBOT or CME executions.

Trades: $14.95 plus ECN fees. Only one base fee for partial fills for orders up to 1000 shares. Otherwise, execution must occur as part of the same order number and at the same price. Price improvement may offset extra commissions.

ECN fees: SOES executions, cancellations, and Island and SelectNet are free. Add $.015/share for Instinet, BTRD, REDI, or Attain.

APPEALING FEATURES: Focus on support.

SUPPORT SYSTEMS: 1-818-242-2119 during market hours and AOL instant messaging: support@daylighttrading.com. Help files on software, chat rooms, 70-page user manual.

OPERATIONAL SYSTEMS: Standard upgrade.

BACKGROUND INFORMATION: Daylight Trading is a division of InvestIn.com, member NASD/SIPC and MSRB.

DREYFUS BROKERAGE SERVICES, INC.

URL: www.edreyfus.com

TYPE OF SITE: Registered full-service broker-dealer in all 50 states.

USERS: Online investors, including short-term traders.

SNAIL MAIL: P.O. Box 48921
          Los Angeles, CA 90048

PHONE: 1-800-421-8395

E-MAIL: support@edreyfus.com

SERVICES: The Dreyfus Remote Access system provides all important stock market information, including portfolio analysis on 20-minute delay.

EXECUTION SYSTEMS: Transactions are cleared through all major national clearing organizations (Depository Trust Co., National Securities Clearing Corp., and Options Clearing Corp.).

FEES:

Account minimum: $1000; $2000 for options; $2000 for margin account.

Quotes: Subscription available to real-time Level II, multiple Nasdaq screens through Data Broadcasting Corp. using Signal Online ($130–$150/month) or StockEdge Online (free with over 5 trades/month; otherwise, $59–$79/month).

Trades: First 3 trades free. $15 flat per online trade up to 10,000 shares. Add $4/order for private data network. No penny stocks online. No Canadian shares.

Broker-assisted: 1-800-888-1708. $29 (includes $4 fee) on trades up to 5000 shares, then add $.01/share.

Mutual funds: 1-800-645-6561. Offers Dreyfus Mutual Fund Online Account Access with over 7000 funds.

IRA accounts: 1-800-843-5466. No annual or setup fee; closing $60.

Options: Online—$1.75/contract ($15 minimum). Broker-assisted—$1.75–$2.25/contract ($29 minimum includes $4 fee).

Margin: Brokers call plus up to 1%.

APPEALING FEATURES: Download personal stock watch and stock prices for import to a PC database management or spreadsheet program. Offers after-hours trading.

SUPPORT SYSTEMS: Toll-free number and e-mail. Glossary. Visitor site, sample screens, and portfolio demo. Research/news through Fast Quotes, Market Watch, News Alert. Financial links page.

OPERATIONAL SYSTEMS: Standard.

BACKGROUND INFORMATION: Established in 1976, Dreyfus Brokerage Services, Inc. (formerly Pacific Brokerage Services, Inc.) is a member firm of the NYSE and other principal U.S. securities exchanges. It is an affiliate of Mellon Bank, N.A.

EQUITY TRADING

URL: www.equitytrading.com

TYPE OF SITE: Day trading firm with trading online and in office.

USERS: Active, self-directed day traders.

SNAIL MAIL: 350 Fifth Avenue, Suite 630
New York, NY 10118

PHONE: 1-877-ETTRADE (388-7233)

E-MAIL: info@equitytrading.com

SERVICES: Three levels of data feed and order entry to select from.

EXECUTION SYSTEMS: Trading executed by Terra Nova Trading LLC, with access to SOES, DOT, and ECNs, including TNTO (ARCA), ISLD, BTRD, REDI, ATTN, and Instinet.

FEES:

Account minimum: $10,000.

Data fees: Three levels—$250/month for RealTick III; $175/month for Fixed RealTick III; $100/month for Lite RealTick III. Fees refundable after 50 transactions per month. $58.50/month for exchange fees. Optional news services include Dow Jones News, $95/month; Comtex News, $25/month; News Watch, $75/month.

Trades: $15/trade up to 1000 shares; then $.015/share over 1000. ECN charges apply.

APPEALING FEATURES: Free day trading and software seminars. In-depth trading workshops

SUPPORT SYSTEMS: Toll-free number and e-mail. Demo and in-house seminar. Instruction manual for downloading. Self-executing movies/tutorials. Margin tutorial, chat room, glossary. Extensive links to research.

OPERATIONAL SYSTEMS: Standard.

BACKGROUND INFORMATION: Equity Trading is a branch of Terra Nova Trading LLC, a registered broker-dealer.

E*TRADE SECURITIES INC.

URL: www.etrade.com

TYPE OF SITE: Full service online discount brokerage offering Web TV compatible. Touch-tone and electronic trading and IPOs.

USERS: All levels of online traders including those doing Level II trading.

SNAIL MAIL: 2400 Geng Road
Palo Alto, CA 94303-3306

P.O. Box 989030
West Sacramento, CA 95798-9030

PHONE: 1-800-ETRADE-1 (387-2331)

SERVICES: Free "membership" to site information without opening account, including 100 free real-time quotes daily. Power E*Trade account with real-time quotes, order execution, and Level II information and IPO offerings. TELE*MASTER®, touchtone and speech recognition telephone investing system, 1-800-STOCKS-1 (1-800-786-2571). Free smart alerts to e-mail or pager. Download to Quicken or Money. Customized portfolio and market watch. Summary statement.

FEES:

Account minimum: $1000. $2000 for margin account. No maintenance fee. Receive $75 credit upon account activation with online application currently available. United Mileage Plus miles for each referral.

Quotes: Free unlimited real-time quotes on log-in during market hours.

Limit and stop order trades: Active investor rebates—$5 discount on 30–74 trades/quarter, $10 discount on 75+ trades/quarter. Not retroactive. Applies only to stock/option trades. Listed—$19.95 for up to 5000 shares; then $.01/share for entire order. OTC—$19.95 for any number of shares.

Market trades: Listed—$14.95 for up to 5000 shares; then $.01/share for entire order. OTC—$19.95 for any number shares. For orders of more than 300 shares, specify AON to avoid charges for multiple executions; $10,000 minimum for naked puts; $25,000 minimum for naked calls.

Touch-tone and direct modem: Same fees as online; plus 12 free connect minutes per trade. Otherwise, $.27/minute.

Broker-assisted: Add $15/trade.

Penny and Canadian stocks: Most available at $19.95 flat rate.

Mutual funds: 4300 to choose from, including 1100 with no loads or transaction fees. $29.95 fee for certain funds.

Options: $20 + $1.75/contract; $29 minimum per trade. Add $15 for broker assistance. Black-Scholes analysis and options leverage analysis services.

IRA accounts: Annual maintenance and setup free.

Margin: Brokers call less ½% to plus 2%.

APPEALING FEATURES: United Airlines Mileage Plus client referral bonus. AOL Rewards sign-up bonus. Free Zacks, Reuters, and Baseline.

SUPPORT SYSTEMS: E*station—24-hour online customer support, online chat. Standard glossary and demo. Commission calculator.

OPERATIONAL SYSTEMS: Standard.

BACKGROUND INFORMATION: Founded as a service bureau in 1982, E*Trade provided online quote and trading services. In 1992, E*TRADE Securities, Inc. was developed as the original all-electronic brokerage. The site, www.etrade.com, was launched in 1996 and is licensed in all 50 states and numerous foreign countries.

FRANKLIN ROSS, INC.

URL: www.franklinross.com

TYPE OF SITE: Full service brokerage specializing in real-time online trading.

USERS: Day traders. Check for registration in your state. Foreign accounts accepted.

SNAIL MAIL: 210 N. University Drive, Suite 705
Coral Springs, FL 233071

PHONE: 1-877-TRADENOW (872-3366)
1-877-YESTRADE (937-8723)

E-MAIL: service@franklinross.com

SERVICES: Point-and-click Level II instant order executions (in as fast as 1.9 seconds).

EXECUTION SYSTEMS: Clearing agent is Southwest Securities, Inc.

FEES:

Standard account: For traders who expect to make fewer than 150 trades per month. $10,000 to open; minimum annual income of $30,000; net worth of $100,000; and 1-year equity investment/ trading experience.

Platinum account: For traders who expect to make more than 150 trades per month. $50,000 to open; minimum annual income of $30,000; net worth of $100,000; and 1-year equity investment/ trading experience.

Account status: If Standard trader makes more than 150 trades per month for 2 consecutive months, account is automatically upgraded to Platinum. Likewise, if Platinum trader makes fewer than 150 trades per month for 2 consecutive months, account is automatically downgraded to Standard.

Data fees: Complete RealTick III trading platform with order entry, Nasdaq Level II, charts, time of sales, Web browser. NYSE, Nasdaq and AMEX exchange fees included. $308.50/month (prorated after 15th of month); Free with Platinum account. Real-time Dow Jones news, $95/month.

Trades: Standard—flat $17.95/trade up to 10,000 shares Nasdaq or up to 2000 shares NYSE/AMEX. Plus $.01/share above 10,000/2000. Platinum—150–250 trades per month, $16.95/trade; 251–350 trades per month, $15.95/trade; 351–450 trades per month, $14.95/trade; 451+ trades per month, $13.95/trade. Plus $.01/share above 10,000/2000.

ECN fees: TNTO, $.0005/share; SOES, $.50/trade; ISLD, $.0025/share; INCA, $.0125/share; SelectNet, $2.50/broadcast trade or $1/preference trade; ATTN, $.005/share; REDI, $.015/share. $.25/canceled trade.

SUPPORT SYSTEMS: Toll-free number, tech FAQs, e-mail.

OPERATIONAL SYSTEMS:

CPU:—Pentium-based 100 MHz processor (Pentium II 233 MHz or better recommended).

Memory:—16 MB RAM (32 MB recommended).

Modem:—28.8k (56k recommended).

Monitor:—14-inch with 640 × 480 dpi resolution as a minimum (17-inch with 800 × 600 dpi resolution recommended).

Operating system:—Windows 95/98 or NT 4.0 workstation with secure Web browser.

BACKGROUND INFORMATION: Franklin Ross is a member of NASD/SIPC.

GRO CORPORATION

URL: www.grotrader.com

TYPE OF SITE: Day trading firm.

USERS: Experienced active traders. Not currently available to residents of HI, ME, or RI.

SNAIL MAIL: 3000 Wesleyan, Suite 390
                          Houston, TX 77027

PHONE: 1-800-852-3862

E-MAIL: info@gro.com

SERVICES: GROtrader™, powered by CyBerTrader™, is an integrated trading environment licensed to GRO Corporation by CyBerCorp Inc. GROtrader operates in real time and offers high-end, high-speed trading systems. "Exclusive brokerage rights" license to Telescan's new search engine, ProSearch Alerts™, which uses filters to identify trading ideas every 5 minutes.

EXECUTION SYSTEMS: Orders routed electronically by GROtrader to the appropriate market maker, ECN, specialist, or exchange. Advanced multiple market execution system features:

- Speed Keys—Use keyboard, not mouse.
- Smart Key—Preprogrammed for routing orders to comply with new rules for day trading.
- Delta Keys—Broadcast orders through SelectNet at inside bid/ask price plus specified delta value of $\cdot 1/16$ to 1 point.
- Auto Cancel—Time-outs after client presets desired time delay.
- Kill All Orders—For all open orders.
- Liquidate All Orders—For all positions should market turn.
- Stop Loss Auto Send—Automatic order send when a predetermined loss amount is reached.
- Basket Trades—Execution to buy or sell against a basket of stocks.
- Close-Out Function—Automatic order to execute remaining shares held in position.
- Buy-In Function—Automatic order to execute remaining shares to complete a full position up to 1000 shares.

FEES:

Account minimum: $25,000 and 6 months' trading experience.

Data fees: $180/month if trading volume is less than 80 tickets per month; free with 80 or more tickets per month.

Trades: $19.95/transaction or $.02/share, whichever is greater, for up to 199 tickets per month. $18.95/transaction or $.019/share, whichever is greater, for 200–299 tickets per month. $17.95/transaction or $.018/share, whichever is greater, for 300–399 tickets per month. $16.95/transaction or $.017/share, whichever is greater, for 400–499 tickets per month. $15.95/transaction or $.016/ share, whichever is greater, for 500–599 tickets per month. $14.95/transaction or $.015/share, whichever is greater, for 600 or more tickets per month.

No maximum ticket size; however, maximum order size is 20,000 shares. No additional base fee for multiple fills within 5 minutes of initial execution.

Additional processing fees may apply to tickets of $1000 and over.

An SEC charge of $.000033/share for all sell orders is added to total commission fee.

ECN fees: SOES, $.50/ticket; $1/ticket; SNET Direct, or Attain Direct, SNET Broadcast, $2.50/ticket; Island Direct, $.0025/share to add or −$.001/share to remove; NYSE (AMRO) or Instinet Direct, $.0125/share; ATTN or INCA, $.015/share; BTRD or TNTO, $.005/share; ISLD or REDI, $.0025. Cancel fee $.25/trade.

Exchange fees: $59.50/month for Nasdaq, NYSE, AMEX, plus option exchanges: $55/month for CME, $60/month for CBOT, $5/month for OPRA.

SUPPORT SYSTEMS: Toll-free number. Research/news includes charting and technical analysis. Daily research available from DLJ and Wall Street Whispers.

Download forms to open account.

EXECUTION SYSTEMS: Standard upgrade.

BACKGROUND INFORMATION: Founded in 1984, GRO Corporation is a member of NASD/SIPC.

INVESTIN.COM SECURITIES CORP.

URL: www.investin.com

TYPE OF SITE: Full service broker/dealer offering IPOs and day trading.

USERS: All levels of online and wireless traders. Not licensed in MA, MN, NH, ND, or Puerto Rico. Licensed in 18 European countries.

SNAIL MAIL: 1950 Stemmons Freeway, Suite 2016
Dallas, TX 75207

PHONE: 1-800-327-1883

E-MAIL: newaccounts@investin.com

SERVICES: Standard online trading with link to Level II quotes. One of few sites offering IPOs online.

EXECUTION SYSTEMS: Clearing firm is Penson Financial Services.

FEES:
   Account minimum: $1000. $2000 for margin account.
   Quotes: Real-time equity quotes for $59/month and real-time equity, future, and option quotes for $130/month through StockEdge and Signal Online. (Use of these services increases account minimum to $2000.)
   Trades: $14.95 + $.01/share for listed market orders; $19.95 for limit, stop, and Nasdaq orders up to 5000 shares. No options, penny, or OTC-BB stocks.
   Broker-assisted: $10 extra per trade.
   Margin: 8.5%.

APPEALING FEATURES: InvestIN.com Securities Corp. is a member of the E Dealer selling group that participates in the online distribution of IPOs.

SUPPORT SYSTEMS: Toll-free number. Tutorials, demo, news, and research.

OPERATIONAL SYSTEMS: Standard.

BACKGROUND INFORMATION: InvestIN.com Securities Corp., a member of NASD/SIPC, has been a licensed broker/dealer since 1996 and provides online financial services through Investin.com, RT2trader.com, and invest.co.uk.

INVESTORS STREET

URL: www.istreet.net

TYPE OF SITE: Day trading firm with online, direct dial-up, and in-office system access.

USERS: Active day traders.

SNAIL MAIL: 1110 Brickell Avenue, Suite 600
Miami, FL 33131

PHONE: 1-888-373-1155

E-MAIL: traders@investors-street.com

SERVICES: Real-time NYSE and Nasdaq Level II stock quotes. Point-and-click order entry with direct access exchanges; trading platforms are RealTick III for charting and decision support and RealTrade for order entry; live scrolling tick by tick, bid/ask, intraday graphs, and daily charts. Alarms with programmable price limits, new highs and lows, volume alerts. Updated Nasdaq Level II MarketMaker screen with time of sales. Portfolio manager window to monitor real-time P&L. Real-time technical studies including moving averages, MACD, momentum, RSI, DMI, stochastics—customizable.

FEES:
> *Trades:* In-house trading—$500/month or 100 tickets per month. ISDN direct trading—$500/month or 200 ticket per month. Internet access—$300/month.
>
> *Fee structure:* $0.02/share with $18 minimum per trade. *Introductory* commission rate is $0.02/share with minimums of $6 for up to 300 shares, $8 for 301–400 shares, and $10 for 401–500 shares.
>
> *ECN fees:* Added to total commission fee. Island, $1 flat fee; Archipelago (includes all SelectNet fees), $0.005/share; SelectNet, $2.50/trade; SuperDOT market orders, $0.005/share; limit orders, $0.0125/share.

APPEALING FEATURES: Confirmations received instantly on order entry screen, along with a record of all orders placed.

SUPPORT SYSTEMS: Glossary. Test drive.

OPERATIONAL SYSTEMS: Direct 128k ISDN access via 128k ISDN point-to-point connection with Istreet-provided hardware and software. Traders wishing access via a 128k ISDN connection will receive the following while trading an Istreet account: Dell OptiPlex GX1 Pentium™ 400 MHz computer with 64 MB of 100 MHz SDRAM; 21-inch monitor; 128k ISDN modem; Windows NT 4.0 workstation; RealTick III trading software.

Standard Internet connection via Pentium-based 166 MHz with 32 MB of RAM, Windows 95/98, and a connection to a reliable ISP is required. Pentium II 233 MHz (or better) with 64 MB RAM, Windows NT 4.0 workstation, and 56k modem with an X2 chipset (such as U.S. Robotics modems) is recommended.

BACKGROUND INFORMATION: In business since 1992, Investors Street is a registered broker-dealer and member of NASD/SIPC.

LIVESTREET.COM

URL: www.livestreet.com

TYPE OF SITE: Order entry agency that does not act as principal and does not make markets in securities. AON, GTC, limit, stop, stop/limit orders, short sales, and option trades permitted. Multiple concurrent orders permitted as long as funds are available.

USERS: Online traders and investors in all states except Nebraska.

SNAIL MAIL: The Franklin Avenue Plaza
1225 Franklin Avenue, Suite 117
Garden City, NY 11530

PHONE: 1-516-873-4200

E-MAIL: clientservice@livestreet.com
questions@livestreet.com
techsupport@livestreet.com

SERVICES: Dynamically updated real-time trading and portfolio management program using RealTick III with live MarketMaker bids/offers and streaming Level II data, order execution, position tracking, Market-Minder, pending order boxes, dynamic customized charts, graphs, and analytics, and optional Dow Jones news. Daily short list.

EXECUTION SYSTEMS: All trades are executed by Terra Nova Trading LLC, a registered broker-dealer. Nasdaq trades on SOES—up to 1000 shares per ticket. Market and limit orders on Nasdaq Level II electronically routed to a Nasdaq market maker for execution. Uses Archipelago (TNTO), an ECN "finder" that seeks the best method of execution. Listed orders are all electronically routed through the CSS to the appropriate specialist's station on the floor of the NYSE or AMEX. Clearing agency is Southwest Securities, Inc., a NYSE-listed company.

FEES:

Account minimum: $10,000 ($1000 in cash) to open; $5000 minimum equity level ($1000 in cash). If equity falls below $5000, trader has 5 business days to re-fund the account to $10,000 or else will be restricted from trading. If equity has not been re-funded by the second-to-last day of the month, the account will be depermissioned and taken off Livestreet.com. Free cash balances above $500 are swept into an interest-bearing account, currently paying 4.5%.

Data fees: $200/month ($2000/year prepaid). Nasdaq Level II, $50/month; execution system, $50/month. Optional exchange fees: CBOT, $60/month; CME, $55/month; Options Price Reporting Authority, $2/month. Extra options: Dow Jones Online News, $75/month; Market Guide Fundamentals and Analysis, $30/month; Comtex News, $50/month. Pricing does not includes Internet service provider (ISP) access charges.

Trades: "Call or e-mail for lowest discount commissions and best executions." Listed—+$0.01/share for any shares over 2000. A single trade/order/ticket generates only one commission regardless of partial or multiple fills.

Options: $35 minimum ticket. 1–5 lot size, $8/option; 6–10 lot size, $6/option; 11+ lot size, $5/option.

ECN fees: ISI listed stocks (NYSE, AMEX), $.008/share; Bloomberg (BTRD), $.005/share; Instinet (INCA), $.0125/share; Island (ISLD), $.0025/trade; Archipelago (TNTO), $.0005/share; Spear Leeds (REDI), $.015/share; Attain (ATTN), $.005/share. Other destinations as charged per trade.

Margin: Equity share price must be $5+. For day trades on margin, cost is *free* if the borrowed portion is sold by close. Otherwise, rate is 8.5%.

SUPPORT SYSTEMS: Instruction in online trading order entry and technical support available by e-mail. Manual available plus on-screen help. Trading screen demo, FAQs.

Open an account by e-mailing online application.

OPERATIONAL SYSTEMS:

CPU: Pentium-based with minimum 166 MHz processor (200+ recommended).

Memory: 32MB RAM (64MB recommended).

Hard disk: minimum 20MB (2GB or even 4GB recommended).

Modem: 64/128k ISDN, 56v90 or 33.6v90 kbps.

Operating system: Win95/98 or NT 4.0 workstation.

Software: Video card, Microsoft Excel spreadsheet or similar, newest Microsoft Explorer.

Hookup: Use a major ISP and connect via MCI, Sprint, IBM, or UUNET.

BACKGROUND INFORMATION: Livestreet.com is a branch of Terra Nova Trading LLC, member NASD/SIPC.

LIVETRADE.COM INC.

URL: www.livetrade.com

TYPE OF SITE: Order entry/execution service that does not act as principal, make markets in securities, receive payment from market makers, or trade against orders. MacIntosh compatible. AON, GTC, limit, stop, stop/limit orders, and short sales permitted. No BB or option trades.

USERS: Online traders in the following states: AL, AK, AR, CA, CO, CT, DC, DE, FL, GA, IA, ID, IL, IN, KS, KY, LA, MA, MD, MI, MS, MT, NC, NM, NE, NJ, NY, NV, OK, OR, PA, RI, SC, SD, TN, TX, UT, VA, VT, WA, WI, WV, and WY.

SNAIL MAIL: 71 Clinton Road
               Garden City, NY 11530

PHONE: 1-516-873-6640
1-877-LIVETRADE (548-3872)

E-MAIL: customerservice@livetrade.com
questions@livetrade.com
techsupport@livetrade.com

SERVICES: Traders have access to live Level II market data, can watch their orders get executed in the market, and can choose routing or let Archipelago choose it. Traders can subscribe to RealTick III full service data feed and order entry, or a customized ticker, or simply order entry software. Free company report and trial subscription to NewsWatch. Daily short list. Site has password military-grade encryption, with high output and input capabilities, and can handle order flow on servers.

EXECUTION SYSTEMS: All trades are executed by Alex Moore & Company, a registered broker-dealer. Nasdaq trader is allowed to choose from SOES, Instinet, SelectNet, Island, SuperDOT, Archipelago, and other ECNs. Listed orders are electronically routed through the CSS to the appropriate specialist's station on the floor of the NYSE or AMEX. Clearing firm is J. B. Oxford & Company.

FEES:

> *Account minimum:* $25,000 equity to open. $7500 minimum account balance ($1000 in cash). Free cash balances above $500 are swept into an interest-bearing account, currently paying 4.5%.

Data fees: Three levels to choose from:

- $324/month, *full data and order entry,* includes the dynamically updated real-time trading and portfolio management program, RealTick III, with live MarketMaker bids/offers and streaming Level II data, order execution, position tracking, MarketMinder, pending order boxes, dynamic customized charts, graphs, and analytics, history, most actives, and alarms. Includes COMTEX News. Fee waived with 50 transactions/month.

- $299/month, *preset data and order entry,* includes custom ticker, Level II data, MarketMaker, order execution, personal interest list, time and sales, charting, history, most actives, alarms, account status, and Web browser. Includes COMTEX News. Fee waived with 50 transactions/month.

- $112.50/month, *LiveLite order entry only,* includes real-time quotes, account information, position list, pending order list, personal interest list, buying power, profit/loss, chat, and Web browser. Fee waived with 20 transactions/month. COMTEX News, $25/month.

Futures quotes are available for viewing at $55/month. Call toll-free customer service for information.

Trades: $19.95 for any trade of 100–10,000 shares. Destination fees extra. $9 extra per call-in trade to toll-free number.

ECN fees: SOES (1000 shares or less, only on Nasdaq), $.25/trade; SOES cancels, $.25 each. SelectNet or Island (unlimited shares on Nasdaq), $1/trade. Bloomberg (BTRD), Spear Leeds (REDI), BRUT, or Attain (ATTN) (unlimited shares on Nasdaq), $.015/share. Instinet (INCA) (unlimited shares), $.015/share. Listed (unlimited shares on listed stocks), $.015/share. ARCHA (minimum $.50/trade), $.0005/share. Other destinations as charged per trade.

APPEALING FEATURES: You can use Macintosh to trade with Livetrade.com using a Windows 95/98 emulator. And you can access your Livetrade.com account, enter buys and sells, and check your portfolio through the Internet using CompuServe, Prodigy, AT&T Worldnet, Concentric, and other reliable services.

SUPPORT SYSTEMS: Order entry and technical support available by e-mail; or by phone Mon–Fri, 8:30 am–5 pm EST. Live chat with customer support or with other clients. Dimensional trade demo. Download order entry software and Windows 95/98 or NT 4.0 from site. Resources page includes links to books and many support sites, such as Briefing.com, Hoover's Online, MarketScience, Pristine Day Trader, Momentum Trader, Home Sweet Trading Floor, Day Traders Stock Picks, Big Charts, and Zacks. Also tutorials on the exchanges, ECNs, and index quotes.

Open an account by e-mailing online application request. Terminations by 18th of month for following-month cancellation, by e-mail: adriana@livetrade.com. Account information: 1-516-873-9370.

OPERATIONAL SYSTEMS:

CPU: Pentium-based with minimum 100 MHz processor (200+ recommended).

Memory: 32MB RAM (64MB recommended).

Hard disk: minimum 20MB (2GB or even 4GB recommended).

Modem: 64/128k ISDN, 56v90 or 33.6v90 kbps.

Operating system: Win95/98 or NT 4.0 workstation with SP3 applied.

Browser: Microsoft Explorer.

Cable modem can be used with a *static* (not dynamic) address.

BACKGROUND INFORMATION: Livetrade.com is a branch of Alex Moore & Company, Inc., member NASD/SIPC.

MARKET WISE TRADING INC.

URL: www.marketwisetrading.com

TYPE OF SITE: Electronic direct access trading company with offices in Denver, Aspen, and Englewood, CO; San Francisco, CA; Tampa, FL; and Baton Rouge, LA. Short sales and option trades permitted.

USERS: All levels, from long-term investors and professional traders to day, swing, and intermediate-term traders.

SNAIL MAIL: 6343 W. 120th Avenue
                      Broomfield, CO 80020

PHONE: 1-877-MKT-TRADE (658-8723)

E-MAIL: accounts@trademarketwise.com

SERVICES: Trading through Internet or phone, using one of 4 software levels:

- Trade Wise Pro is designed for trading less than 5 times a month. Includes real-time quotes, time and sales, technical studies, and intraday, daily, and weekly charting ability for making trading decisions. Dynamically updated real-time position and account managers.
- Trade Wise Elite adds one Level II screen, allowing trader to see the depth of the bid and offer in real time.
- Trade Wise Elite Plus system adds the ability to utilize Level II information on two equities at the same time and provides the additional market information needed for simultaneously trading multiple equities.
- Trade Wise Master provides unlimited Level II market information on many different equities at the same time.

EXECUTION SYSTEMS: Software platform centered around powerful E-DAT execution. An execution control panel places trades on the primary exchange market or ECN identified by the trader: NYSE trades on Super-DOT; Nasdaq market, limit, and smart trades on SOES, ECNs, SelectNet, and Archipelago. Clearing agent is Penson Financial Services, Inc.

FEES:

Account minimum: $5000 to open Trade Wise Pro account. $25,000 for other account levels.

Data fees: Nonpro exchange fees for U.S. equities and options are in-cluded. Pro service—$160/month; free with 25 trades (50 transactions) per month. Elite service—$260/month; free with 38 trades (75 transactions) per month. Elite Plus service—$285/month; free with 50 trades (100 transactions) per month. Master service—$325/month; free with 50 trades (100 transactions) per month. All software discounts are based on a looking-back system, with account adjustments made in the following month.

Trades: $23 flat fee per transaction, plus pass-through fees: SEC $.0000333 × principal amount. SOES, $.50/transaction. Direct ECNs (ISLD, ARCA), $1/transaction. SuperDot (NYSE/AMEX), $.01/share on executions up to 2088 shares; $.015/share on executions over 2088 shares. Add $10 for all phone orders. $65/month for Turbo options, $55/month for CME futures, $4/month for AMEX, and $60/month for CBOT.

APPEALING FEATURES: Research center offering free domestic/international market summary graphs and a detailed quote/symbol lookup or 20-stock fast quote. Client research includes market movers, broker reports, charting, buy/hold/sell, splits, and short list.

SUPPORT SYSTEMS: Free link to stock quotes on every page. Market Wise book store, Market Wise calendar of seminars, and free trial registration to chat room. Link to "Market Wise Stock Trading School LLC" Web site, an independent E-DAT training facility.

Open an account by completing, printing, and mailing online application and signature forms. When account application is approved, you will receive account number by phone and can then submit required deposit. When deposit clears, you will receive trade approval. Download software from online site.

OPERATIONAL SYSTEMS:
CPU: Pentium II 300 MHz.
Memory: 96MB RAM.
Hard disk: 3.2 GB with 3.5" 1.44 MB floppy disk drive.
Operating system: Windows NT 4.0 workstation with service pack pcANYWHERE32 v8.0 client.

Monitor: If split monitors are used, Appian, STB, or Color Graphix installation is suggested.

BACKGROUND INFORMATION: Market Wise Trading Inc., member NASD/SIPC, was formed by David S. Nassar, author of *How to Get Started in Electronic Day Trading.*

MAX TRADE LLC

URL: www.maxtrading.com

TYPE OF SITE: Day trading site with online, remote, and in-office system access.

USERS: All levels, including day traders.

SNAIL MAIL: 560 Kirts Boulevard, Suite 118
Troy, MI 48084

PHONE: 1-248-362-2650
1-888-741-8733

E-MAIL: mailbox@maxtrading.com

SERVICES: MaxPRO, MaxPLUS, and MaxPREMIER all use RealTick III and provide access to Archipelago. Real-time order entry and electronic execution program with MarketMaker bids/offers, position minder, hot keys, board view, tickers, alarms, MarketMinder, and MultiQuote. Options are offered on a call-in basis. Trading screen customization and trading simulation demos. Free company research with symbol lookup on home page. Trader's reports access from home page directory.

EXECUTION SYSTEMS: All trades are executed by Terra Nova Trading LLC, a registered broker-dealer, on an order routing system that allows traders access to at least 4 ECNs: SOES, SelectNet, Archipelago—TNTO (ARCA), and Island—ISLD. Also, Instinet—INCA (phone orders only), CSS SuperDOT, Bloomberg Trade Book—BTRD, and Spear Leads Tradebook—REDI. Clearing firm is Southwest Securities, Inc., a NYSE-listed company.

Max Trade offers two options for data connections: standard reliable Internet connection for traders that require a moderate amount of data with conservative trading practices, and special remote connections for highly active traders.

FEES:

Account minimum: $10,000 equity to open. Margin account rate currently 8%. Pays 4% on available cash balances.

Data fees: MaxPRO—$100/month, limited RealTick III. MaxPLUS—$175/month, includes fixed RealTick III plus Nasdaq Level II.

MaxPREMIER—$250/month. RealTick III plus multiple customizable Level II windows. Data fees are waived on accounts that execute 50 trades or more per month. Fees charged first week of each month; discounts retroactive to first trade of month and credited to following month. Optional monthly subscription fees for CME futures, $50; CBOT futures, $65; Turbo options, $5; NewsWatch, $75 (include Zacks for an extra $15).

Trades: Trade commissions do not include exchange/ECN destination charges. $21.95/trade for up to 50 trades per month; $20.95/trade for 51–100 trades per month; $19.95/trade for 100+ trades per month.

APPEALING FEATURES: Review of recently released financial books on trading and related subjects. Link to Amazon.com for purchase.

SUPPORT SYSTEMS: Toll-free customer service and chat room (download mIRC software from site for other financial chat rooms). Comprehensive resources links to general market info, training, market news, technical news, alerts.

In-office training course customized to each trader's specific training curve and ability, including risk management. All students use training computers on a daily basis to test information covered. Class runs 6:30 pm–9 pm for 3 evenings. Training materials are free for class participants, and are available for nominal costs for other customers. Call for availability and pricing.

Open an account by downloading all pertinent application forms.

OPERATIONAL SYSTEMS:

CPU: Pentium-based processor.

Memory: 32MB RAM.

Modem: minimum 28.8k.

Operating system: Win95/98 or NT 4.0 workstation.

Browser: Microsoft Explorer 4.0.

Hookup: Use a major ISP and connect via MCI, Sprint, IBM, or UUNET.

BACKGROUND INFORMATION: Max Trading, formed in 1997, is a branch of Terra Nova Trading LLC, member NASD/SIPC.

PACIFIC DAY TRADING, INC.

URL: www.day-trade.com

TYPE OF SITE: Day trading brokerage with remote and in-office trading.

USERS: Active traders.

SNAIL MAIL: Town & Country Village
2980 Stevens Creek Boulevard, Suite 410B
San Jose, CA 95128

PHONE: 1-408-557-9000

E-MAIL: customerservice@day-trade.com

SERVICES: Nasdaq Level II or NYSE real-time data along with Windows software package. Customizable, dynamic MarketMinder snapshot window and multiple real-time ticker view windows. TicketMinder.

EXECUTION SYSTEMS: Clearing company is Southwest Securities, Inc.

FEES:

Account minimum: Check with site.

Onsite fees: $350/month onsite subscription service allows real-time trading on Nasdaq Level II or NYSE. Fee waived with 10 fills per day, averaged over a month. Service provides connection to ultra high-speed Windows NT workstations; load-balanced servers to help ensure against server slowdown; 200MHz Intel Pentium processor with 64MB RAM; dual 17" monitors with special split-screen video card; Pacific Day Trading workstation software; and simulator trading software.

Remote fees: User has own ISP. Fixed-page RealTick, $175/month + exchange fees. Full-page RealTick, $250/month + exchange fees.

Trades: $.02295/share with $22.95 minimum per fill. Fill is up to 1000 shares of stock at one price level.

Exchange fees: NYSE, $5.25/month; AMEX, $3.25/month; Nasdaq Level II, $50/month; Nasdaq Level I, $4/month; Options, $5/month; CME, $55/month; CBOT, $60/month.

ECN fees: $.008/share for ISI (NYSE); $.0129/share for Instinet;

$2.50/fill for SelectNet; $.0025/share for Island; $.50/fill for SOES; $.015/share for other ECNs; $.50/fill for ARCA.

APPEALING FEATURES: In-house trading for retail customers.

SUPPORT SYSTEMS: Basic Training Boot Camp through Electronic Day Trading Services (cost recovered by discounted per share trade fee).

OPERATIONAL SYSTEMS: Standard upgrade.

BACKGROUND INFORMATION: Pacific Day Trading, member NASD/SIPC, is a branch of Terra Nova Trading LLC.

POLAR TRADING INC.

URL: www.polartrading.com

TYPE OF SITE: Browser-based market/limit (only) order entry system. No online futures, funds, or bonds. Short sales permitted.

USERS: Active traders and remote traders who routinely make more than 10 trades per month and are looking for high growth and risk. No Canadian residents.

SNAIL MAIL: 49 Macomb Place, Suite 200
Mt. Clemens, MI 48043

PHONE: 1-810-463-0140
1-888-771-7657

E-MAIL: customerservice@polartrading.com

SERVICES: Provides real-time quotations. Traders view holdings and place orders directly through Web browser without additional software. "Cool Tools"—Polar's online Pivot Point calculator, sound files, and Island monitor. In-house trading floor features 32 state-of-the-art terminals and twin large-screen monitors with up-to-the-minute stock and securities activity.

Trading is done on 3 software levels:
- Polar Trader (full- and fixed-page versions)—includes real-time Level II MarketMaker and time of sales data. Includes Turbo options if you subscribe to CBOT or OPRA. Customizable charting, instantaneous order entry and trade confirmations, along with real-time position management, interest list, option quotes, and integrated Web browsers.
- Full Polar Trader—includes Turbo options.
- Polar Trader Jr.—the order execution system of Polar Trader without Level II or time of sales. Primarily for traders currently using other third-party stock analysis applications.

EXECUTION SYSTEMS: All trades are executed by Terra Nova Trading LLC, a registered broker-dealer, on an electronic order routing system through SOES, Archipelago, other ECNs, and SuperDOT linked to Nasdaq, NYSE, and AMEX. All transactions cleared through Southwest Securities, Inc., a NYSE-listed company.

FEES:

Account minimum: $5000 equity to open.

Data fees: Polar Trader Jr.—$125/month; free with 20 trades per month. Polar Trader "Fixed Page"—$230/month for 1–19 trades per month; $30/month for 20–49 trades per month; free with 50 trades per month. Polar Trader "Full"—$300/month for 1–19 trades per month; $100/month for 20–49 trades per month; free with 50 trades per month. Optional monthly subscription fees for CME futures, $55; CBOT futures, $60; OPRA, $2. Software subscription includes exchange fees.

Trades: Trade commissions do not include ECN destination charges. For novice traders, a special commission of $.05/share ($5 per 100-share lot) is available for 60 days from account activation and includes seminars, monthly classes, and weekly chat. Otherwise, $22.95/trade for 1–19 trades per month; $21.95/trade for 20–49 trades per month; $19.95/trade for 50–99 trades per month; $17.95/trade for 100–199 trades per month; $15.95/trade for 200–399 trades per month; $14.95/trade for 400+ trades per month.

APPEALING FEATURES: Polar Trading's *free* Internet Continuing Education (ICE™) program is a fully interactive classroom and Internet-based self-paced training curriculum with extensive training modules for any skill level. Course modules present an overview of short-term and other possible strategies for successful day traders. Seminars about securities trading and financial management are run by leading money managers.

Certain modules are free to anyone; other modules are available only to Polar members and can be accessed at their discretion. Members can also register and pay online ($19.95 each) for modules that are not free.

SUPPORT SYSTEMS: Free NewsAlert, Baseline, The Street.com, Polar Analytics. and end-of-day and margin reports. Toll-free and e-mail customer service as well as PolarChat room. Comprehensive resources downloads, links to news, and bookstore. Glossary and FAQs.

Open an account by downloading application questionnaire and signature forms; takes about 45 minutes to complete.

OPERATIONAL SYSTEMS:

CPU: Pentium-based processor.

Memory: 32MB RAM.

Modem: Minimum 28.8k.

Operating system: Win95/98 or NT 4.0 workstation.

Software: Microsoft Explorer 4.0, Adobe Acrobat.

Hookup: Dedicated phone line, major ISP, and connection via MCI, Sprint, IBM, or UUNET.

BACKGROUND INFORMATION: Polar Trading, formed in 1997, is a branch of Terra Nova Trading LLC, member NASD/SIPC.

RML TRADING

URL: www.rmltrading.com

TYPE OF SITE: Day trading site capable of Level II trading.

USERS: Active day traders.

SNAIL MAIL: 40 Lake Bellevue
Suite 168
Bellevue, WA 98005

PHONE: 1-888-765-4403

E-MAIL: info@rmltrading.com

SERVICES: RML Power Trader is a flexible trading platform using HyperFeed, a digital market data feed. Power Trader includes Nasdaq Level II screens, technical studies and charts, alarms, snap quotes, fundamentals, hot keys, BoardView, MarketMaker data, time and sales, MarketMinder, ticker, and RML's order entry system and StockCam.

EXECUTION SYSTEMS: SuperDOT system used exclusively for executing listed securities, through RichMark Capital Corporation.

FEES:
Account minimum: $10,000 to open; $50,000 recommended.
Data fees: RML Power Trader software, $250/month plus nonpro exchange fees of $50. Software fees waived after 100 round-trip trades per month. News, $75/month. Options quotes, $50/month.
Trades: Listed/market—$14.95. OTC—$14.95 + $.01/share for listed. SOES market/limit—$14.95. ISLD bid/offer—$14.95. Inside order book on ARCH—$14.95 + other ECNs.

APPEALING FEATURES: Sophisticated support for software and trading.

SUPPORT SYSTEMS: Live video/audio customer support, StockCam. In-office training once a week. Video demo of software. Day trader course for $995.

OPERATIONAL SYSTEMS: Web browser (Internet Explorer 4.01) and Windows media player available for free download.

Operating system: Windows 95/98 or NT workstation.

CPU: Pentium-based 133MHz processor.

Memory: 64MB RAM (128MB recommended).

Hard drive: At least 2.0 GB recommended with standard 3.5″ floppy drive and CD-ROM 8× speed (minimum).

Sound card: SoundBlaster recommended or any Windows-compatible sound card and speakers.

Video card: Windows-compatible with 2MB of RAM, capable of 1024 × 768 dpi resolution in thousands of colors.

Monitor: 17-inch .28MM dpi capable of displaying at 1280 × 1024 dpi resolution (1024 × 768 dpi minimum).

Keyboard: Windows-compatible 104 key.

Mouse: PC two-button.

Modem: 56.6k connection or faster (ISDN line); highly recommended for StockCam viewers.

BACKGROUND INFORMATION: Founded by Robert Luecke, RML Trading, Inc. is a member of NASD and SIPC.

RT DAY TRADING

URL: www.rttrading.com

TYPE OF SITE: Online day trading firm. Also offers electronic trading via PDA.

USERS: Active traders.

SNAIL MAIL: 1950 Stemmons Freeway, Suite 2016
                             Dallas, TX 75207

PHONE: 1-800-327-1883

SERVICES:
- RT2 Trader orders are tracked in real time through the account management system using the latest PC Windows technology. System shows when each order is executed, at what price, and who the counterparty is.
- Trading packages include RT2 (remote trading in real time; adapted from TradeCast), RealTick III, and Mercenary Analytics.
- RealTick III breaks down all the available market data and displays it functionally and easily for quick referencing.
- Mercenary Analytics package functions in two parts—Hawkeye and Sniper. Hawkeye creates a basket of 100 stocks to monitor and indicates stocks that merit closer inspection. Sniper sifts through all the available market data for a target and breaks the data down into 12 different price-influencing sectors.

EXECUTION SYSTEMS: Clearing firm is Penson Financial Services.

FEES:
Account minimum: $10,000.
Data fees:
- $300/month for RT2 Trader with a Nasdaq Level II screen and order routing to ECNs.
- $300/month for RealTick III with real-time streaming market data and live executions.
- $79.95/month for Mercenary Analytics.
  $100 rebate if trades total 51–75/month. Free software if trades total 76–400/month. Free software and Mercenary if trades exceed 400/month or 100,000 shares traded per month.

Trades: $7.95/trade for up to 100 trades per month; $6.95/trade for over 100 trades per month. Plus $.02/share for up to 25,000 shares per trade; $.015/share for 25,001–50,000 shares per trade; $.01/share for 50,001–100,000 shares per trade; $.005/share for 100,001+ shares per trade. Maximum commission charge is $19.95/trade.

Exchange/ECN fees: Additional.

APPEALING FEATURES: Software supports all levels of trading. Site has referral link to InvestIn.Com for nonday traders.

SUPPORT SYSTEMS: Toll-free number. Trading seminars. Links to news and research. Traders Press bookstore.

OPERATIONAL SYSTEMS:

CPU: Minimum Pentium-based 166 MHz processor (Pentium II 233 for RealTick III and Pentium II 266 for Mercenary).

Memory: 64MB with 100MB free disk space.

Operating system: Windows 95/98 or NT.

Modem: 56k. "Top end" ISPs such as MCI or AT&T are needed to function efficiently. Services such as AOL cannot be used.

Monitor: Dual-screen setup with 17-inch monitors—the "ultimate" for trading online.

BACKGROUND INFORMATION: RT Day Trading is the online day trading site for InvestIn.Com Securities, Inc.

STOXNOW.COM
(FORMERLY DIRECT NET TRADING)

URL: www.stoxnow.com

TYPE OF SITE: Agency for online day trading.

USERS: Active day traders.

SNAIL MAIL: 7464 E Tierra Buena Lane, #203
               Scottsdale, AZ 85260

PHONE: 1-877-872-3372

E-MAIL: info@STOXNOW.com

SERVICES: Online trading system offers instant executions, combined with live Level II quotes, charting, tickers, alerts. Short sales are routed through staff for approval.

EXECUTION SYSTEMS: Traders may preference their order routing. Penson Financial Services is the clearing agent.

FEES:

Account minimum: $5000.

Data fees: $340/month for ProTrader. Rebate of $40 for 10 tickets/month or $300 for 76 tickets/month.

Trades: $16.95/ticket for up to 100 trades per month; $15.95/ticket for 101–200 trades per month; $14.95/ticket for over 200 trades per month. Add $.008/share for listed trades. Only one base fee for partial fills for orders up to 2000 shares. Otherwise, execution must occur as part of the same order number and at the same price. Price improvement may offset extra commissions.

Options: $25 min./ticket. $25 + $1.75/contract.

ECN fees: SOES $.50/trade, Island and SelectNet are $1.00/trade. Add $.005/share for Archipelago.

SUPPORT SYSTEMS: E-mail support. Extensive help with learning Real-Tick III trading software. One-on-one training available in Scottsdale office.

OPERATIONAL SYSTEMS:

CPU: Pentium-based with minimum 133 MHz processor (166 MHz or greater recommended).

Memory: Minimum 32 MB of RAM (64MB recommended). Available hard disk space should be no less than 20 MB.

Modem: 64/128k ISDN, 56 or 33.6 kbps.

Monitor: Largest possible monitor (or multiple monitors) with 2MB video card.

BACKGROUND INFORMATION: Stoxnow.com is a division of InvestIn .Com Securities Corp., member NASD/SIPC and MSRB.

TERRA NOVA TRADING LLC

URL: www.terranovatrading.com

TYPE OF SITE: Day trading site with streaming real-time Level II data and direct access order entry. No online BB, options, or futures trades.

USERS: Active traders. Foreign accounts accepted.

SNAIL MAIL: 100 S. Wacker Drive, Suite 202
Chicago, IL 60606

PHONE: 1-800-258-5409

E-MAIL: Full phone/e-mail directory available through "Contact Us" site page.

SERVICES: Terra Nova Trader is a Windows-based, dynamically updated real-time trading and portfolio management system adapted from RealTick III, with direct access to the Archipelago ECN. Features user-customized design trading screens.

EXECUTION SYSTEMS: Terra Nova offers comprehensive order routing and electronic interface with ARCA, INCA, ISLD, SOES, and several DOT systems. Traders view live orders and real-time margin calculations to determine funds availability before submitting orders to an exchange. Clearing firm is Southwest Securities, Inc., a NYSE-listed company. Does not sell order flow.

FEES:

Account minimum: $3000 to open; $5000 recommended. Margin interest rate currently 7.7%.

Data fees: Terra Nova Trader Full—$250/month; unlimited product configuration software package includes technical studies for charting and historical data review. TNTrader Fixed, (limited version for a single stock)—$175/month. Nasdaq Level II quotes—$50/month. A software fee rebate of 50% is offered when volume is between 20 and 49 trades per month, and software fees are waived for 50+ trades per month. Subscription links provided to Mercenary and OptiMark.

Commission structure: Tiered commissions are based on monthly volume. Volume discounts are retroactively applied to entire month and credits are issued the following month. (For purposes of calculation, a month ends on the third business day before the last Friday.) Partial or multiple fills do not carry additional commissions.

Trades: $22.50/ticket for 1–19 trades per month; $21.95/ticket for 20–49 trades per month; $19.95/ticket for 50–99 trades per month; $17.95/ticket for 100–199 trades per month; $16.95/ticket for 200–399 trades per month; $14.95/ticket for 400+ trades per month. A ticket equals 2000 shares; add $.015/share for any trade over 2000.

ECN fees: Listed stocks (ABN AMRO/ISI), $.008/share. SOES execution, $.50/trade; SOES cancellation, $.25/trade. Bloomberg (BTRD) or AllTech (ATTN), $.005/share. Instinet (INCA), $.0125/share. Island (ISLD) or Spear Leeds (REDI), $.0025/trade. Archipelago (ARCA), $.0005/share. NexTrade PIM Globa Equities (NTRD), $.015/share. SelectNet Broadcast (SNET), $2.50/trade. Preferred (ARCA), $1/trade. Brass Utility (BRUT), $1.50/trade for up to 199 shares; $3/trade for 200–299 shares; $4/trade for 300 shares and over. Strike Technologies (STRK), no fees.

APPEALING FEATURES: Individual users can create and save an unlimited number of custom pages, changing background and text colors and customizing individual window preferences. Online design demo for chart, table, ticker, Turbo options, MarketMinder, MarketMaker, time of sale, Multiquote, stocks, market profile, trade manager, and Web browser screens.

SUPPORT SYSTEMS: Toll-free technical (1-800-228-4216) and trading (1-800-452-6294) support Mon–Fri, 8 am–6 pm EST. After-hours trading desk support (1-312-960-1314) and Instinet help (1-312-960-1354). Trading software is downloaded from site, and download page covers installation tutorial. Includes Web browser. Help manual and Adobe Acrobat can be downloaded. Margin tutorial. Demo and FAQs. Subscription links provided to NewsWatch and Stock Tax.

Open an account by downloading online application and all forms to speed the process.

OPERATIONAL SYSTEMS:

CPU: Pentium-based.

Memory: 32MB RAM.

Modem: Minimum 28.8k.

Operating system: Win95/98 or NT.

Browser: Microsoft Explorer 4.0.

Hookup: Dual-channel ISDN Internet access with MCI, UUNET, Sprint, or IBM (with a backup ISP) strongly recommended.

BACKGROUND INFORMATION: Terra Nova Trading, member NASD/SIPC, was founded in 1994 and codeveloped the Archipelago ECN with Townsend Analytics.

TREND TRADER

URL: www.trendtrader.com

TYPE OF SITE: Online day trading firm with direct access order entry.

USERS: Active day traders.

SNAIL MAIL: 15030 N. Hayden Road, Suite 120
Scottsdale, AZ 85260

PHONE: 1-888-32-TREND (328-7363)

SERVICES: Order routing and execution.

EXECUTION SYSTEMS: Trading through Nasdaq, SOES, and several ECNs: INTO, ISLD, BTRD, REDI, ATTN, Instinet.

FEES:

Account minimum: $15,000 to open; $10,000 to maintain.

Trades: Less than 201 trades per month—$25/ticket. 201–400 trades per month—$22/ticket. 401–600 trades per month, $18/ticket. 600+ trades per month—$15/ticket. Commissions include any additional fees for SOES, ECNs, and SelectNet.

TORS Elite: Order routing to SOES, ECNs, and DOT, Level II Market-Maker screen, online P&L. Includes NYSE, AMEX, Nasdaq Level II, and OPRA: 80 trades (40 round trips), $315/month.

TORS Wall Street: Order routing to SOES, ECNs, and DOT, Level II MarketMaker screen, online P&L. Includes NYSE, AMEX, Nasdaq Level II, and OPRA: 40 trades (20 round trips), $240/month.

TORS Express: Order routing to SOES, ECNs, and DOT, online P&L. Includes NYSE, AMEX, Nasdaq Level I and OPRA: 20 trades (10 round trips), $115/month.

SUPPORT SYSTEMS: Free 1-day demo of TORS software at Scottsdale day trading facility. Free technical support.

OPERATIONAL SYSTEMS: Standard.

BACKGROUND INFORMATION: TREND TRADER is a registered broker-dealer with the SEC; member NASD/SIPC.

WALL STREET ACCESS

URL: www.wsaccess.com

TYPE OF SITE: Full service brokerage firm capable of Level II online trading.

USERS: Active day traders; institutional money managers.

SNAIL MAIL: Online Sales Department
17 Battery Place
New York, NY 10004

PHONE: 1-800-925-5781

E-MAIL: sales@online.wsaccess.com

SERVICES: Place Internet market, limit, and stop orders on equities; market and limit orders on options. Cancel or change open orders; review the status of orders. Receive complimentary research (TheStreet .com, Zacks, and Briefing.com). Obtain real-time quotes during market hours, view account positions and review up to 6 months of trading activity. For touch-tone orders, Enter market or limit and receive real-time quotes for stocks, options, mutual funds, and leading market indicators during market hours. Obtain account information and receive faxes of your positions, balances, and open and executed orders. Direct dial-up access from PC, 24 hours a day.

EXECUTION SYSTEMS: Clearing company is BT Alex. Brown.

FEES:

Account minimum: None, no software fees, and no connection charges.

Trades: Online, touch-tone, or direct dial-up—1–5000 shares, $45 flat fee; 5000+ shares, $.02/share. Place order with a trader—1–5000 shares, $45 flat fee; 5000+ shares, $.02/share.

Options: Contracts less than $1—$40 + $1.50/contract. Contracts $1 or above—$40 + $2/contract.

Bonds: $40 + $2/bond.

Active trader rebates: For Omega Research or Data Broadcasting Corp. (DBC) subscription, call 1-800-925-5781. Rates are based on annual prepay bill plan. Monthly rebates apply as long as you are a DBC subscriber. Commissions must total as follows in equities or in options each month:

$225 in equities, $600 in options—rebate is $90/month for StockEdge, StockEdge Online, or Quo Trek.

$450 in equities, $1200 in options—rebate is $199 up to 12 months for TradeStation 2000, OptionStation 2000, or Radar Screen 2000; $180/month for Signal; $150/month for Signal Online; $217/month for BMI.

$600 Equities, $1,600 in Options—rebate is $299 up to 16 months for ProSuite 2000.

Margin: Rates subject to change based on brokers call. Net balance $0–$29,999, 9.9%; $30,000–$59,000, 9.5%; $60,000–$99,999, 9.0%; $100,000, 8.5%; $499,999, 8.45%. Credit balances in excess of $2000 accrue interest at 2.5% below the BT Alex. Brown call rate.

APPEALING FEATURES: Commission calculator.

SUPPORT SYSTEMS: Toll-free number and e-mail. Interactive demo. TheStreet.com news service. BT Alex. Brown Morning Notes at BT Alex. Briefing.com; Zacks Wall Street Source; EDGAR Online. Link to quotes, charts, news, and commentary from CBS MarketWatch.

Open an account by downloading forms or request forms by e-mail.

OPERATIONAL SYSTEMS: Adobe Acrobat for forms.

BACKGROUND INFORMATION: Founded in 1981, Wall Street Access, member NASD/SIPC, is not a soliciting broker and does not make investment recommendations.

WEB STREET SECURITIES

URL: www.webstreet.com

TYPE OF SITE: Online discount brokerage with direct access. Web TV compatible.

USERS: Active day traders. Foreign accounts accepted.

SNAIL MAIL: 510 Lake Cook Road, Suite #400
             Deerfield, IL 60015

PHONE: 1-800-WEB TRADE (932-8722)

E-MAIL: customerservice@webstreetsecurities.com

SERVICES: Order entry capable of Level I and Level II trading. Unlimited real-time quotes. Instant executions on most marketable orders (6–10 seconds). Unlimited access to Baseline company and industry profiles. Online pop-up confirmations; monitoring of 10 separate watch lists (up to 10 positions each). Premium services include one-click trading, Nasdaq Level II, and streaming, self-updating quotes.

EXECUTION SYSTEMS: Clearing agent is U.S. Clearing Corp.

FEES:
  Account minimum: None. $2000 margin account.
  Quotes: Real-time, $29.95/month; Nasdaq Level II, $50/month.
  Limit/market orders: $14.95 for any online trade.
  Nasdaq: Any listed stock, $14.95 for less than 1000 shares.
  Broker-assisted: $24.95.
  Mutual funds: $25/trade.
  Penny stocks: Available through SOES (not SelectNet) at same rates as
     above.
  IRA account: Free with $10,000 balance.
  Margin: $7\frac{1}{4}\%$–$8\frac{1}{2}\%$.

SUPPORT SYSTEMS: Full contact directory. Security encryption. Baseline news.

OPERATIONAL SYSTEMS: Netscape Navigator or Internet Explorer ID password and execution password recommended.

BACKGROUND INFORMATION: Web Street Securities is a member SIPC/NASD.

Direct Access
Trading Sites

Designed for experienced day traders, the following sites offer the widest access to the markets.

1-800-DAYTRADE.COM

URL: www.1800daytrade.com

TYPE OF SITE: Deep discount broker offering day trading before, during, and after market hours.

USERS: Active day traders. Check for registration in your state. Foreign accounts accepted.

SNAIL MAIL: 17370 Preston Road, Suite 470
Dallas, TX 75252

PHONE: 1-800-329-8723

E-MAIL: customer service@1800daytrade.com
new accounts@1800daytrade.com
tech support@1800daytrade.com

SERVICES: Wireless trading. Daily short list. Proprietary software for real-time Level I and Level II MarketMaker trading.

EXECUTION SYSTEMS: With software, trader watches order execution. All transactions cleared through Penson Financial Services, Inc.

FEES:

Account minimum: $5000 to open (Investor), $25,000 for margin account (Gold/Platinum).

Data fees: Futures exchange data, $65/month; Turbo option quotes, $6/month.

Millennium Trading Gold: $225/month (free with 50 trades per month). Includes Level I quotes, point-and-click order entry. Special offer of first 5 trades free within 5 days of account activation.

Millennium Trading Platinum: $299/month (free with 50 trades per month). Includes Level II quotes, real-time charts, balances, P&L, point-and-click order entry. Special offer of first 10 trades free within 5 days of account activation.

Trades: Millennium investor accounts: $14.95/trade, plus $.02/share over 2000 shares for listed securities. Millennium Gold/Platinum accounts: $19.95/ticket (+$.01/sh over 2,000 shs)

Phone-in orders: Add $10/trade.

After-hours trades: Add $.05/share.

Wireless trading: Requires investor account.

Option contracts: $21/ticket plus $2.50/contract; minimum $30/order.

Exchange/ECN fees: No charge for SOES, ATTN, SNET, ARCA, ISLD, TNTO. Add $.015/share for BTRD or INCA; $.01/share for AMEX/NYSE. All other exchange fees are included.

No extra charge for partial or multiple fills.

APPEALING FEATURES: Before-and-after market hours trading through Instinet; add $.04/share to Gold or Platinum account.

SUPPORT SYSTEMS: Live one-on-one Web customer service, live chat, free in-office one-day training class. Download software demo.

Open account by downloading forms and mailing.

OPERATIONAL SYSTEMS:

CPU: Pentium II or higher.

Memory: 64MB RAM/SDRAM or PC100 6ns.

Hard disk: 2GB or higher.

Video: 4MB PCI video card (any brand).

Modem: Minimum 56k v.90 with cable connection (there is also DSL and ISDN).

Operating system: Win95/98 or NT 4.0 workstation.

BACKGROUND INFORMATION: 1-800-DayTrade.Com is a member of NASD/SIPC.

A.B. WATLEY

URL: www.abwatley.com

TYPE OF SITE: Deep discount broker-dealer.

USERS: All levels of online traders, including direct access and after-hours.

SNAIL MAIL: 40 Wall Street
New York, NY 10005

PHONE: 1-888-ABWATLEY (229-2853)

E-MAIL: newaccount@abwatley.com

SERVICES: All levels of software accounts with tiered pricing. Touch-tone trading with Level 1 service. Dedicated port service (DPS), based on frame-relay telecommunications technology, allows unlimited connection time for a fixed monthly cost of $300.

EXECUTION SYSTEMS: Level 1 service goes to Watley trader desk. Levels 2, 3, and 4 are directed by trader. Options are routed to the RAES system. All transactions cleared by Penson Financial Services, Inc.

FEES:

Account minimum: Level 1—$3000. Levels 2, 3, 4—$20,000. No extra charge for broker-assisted trades.

Data fees: $50/month for Turbo options; $95/month for Dow Jones News. Other detailed company and industry reports at varying nominal costs.

Watley Trader: $50/month. Free unlimited real-time quotes. $9.95/trade up to 5000 shares. Over 5000 shares, add $.01/share for entire order (e.g., $109.95 for 10,000 shares). No ECN fees. Touch-tone (1-800-215-9267), extra $2/trade, $.01/quote. Extra $15 for broker assistance. Phone-in trades will not be assessed any charges if Web site is inaccessible due to A.B. Watley downtime during market hours.

Ultimate Trader Silver: $75/month (free with 25+ trades per month). No charts or Level II quotes.

Ultimate Trader Gold: $150/month ($125/month for 10–24 trades;

$75/month for 25–49 trades; free with 50+ trades per month). No Level II quotes.

Ultimate Trader Platinum: $300/month ($250/month for 10–24 trades; $200/month for 25–49 trades; free with 50+ trades per month). Includes RealTick III's dynamic real-time, streaming exchange-fed quotes; Nasdaq Level II color-coded MarketMaker screens; complete list of buyers and sellers above and below market. Charts include daily, weekly, monthly, stochastics, moving average and trend lines, point and figure, candlesticks, and overlays.

Commissions structure: 1–9 trades per month, $23.95/trade; 10–24 trades per month, $22.95/trade; 25–49 trades per month—$20.95/trade; 50–99 trades per month, $19.95/trade; 100–199 trades per month, $18.95/trade. Aggressive commission discounts for volume above 199 trades per month. For all listed orders greater than 2000 shares, add $.01/share for the excess per trade. For all Nasdaq orders of 10,000 shares or more, add $.01/share for the excess per trade.

ECN fees: Extra $.015/share for INCA, REDI, TNTO, ATTN; extra $.005/share for BTRD; $1.25/ticket for SelectNet. New ECN charges will be applied at prevailing rates.

Mutual funds: No-load funds—principal amount/fees per fund up to $25,000, $40; $25,001 to $50,000, $50; $50,001 and over, $60.

IRA accounts: $30/year; free setup; closing $50.

Options: $30 + $1.75/contract; minimum $35. Direct access to RAES (via Internet) and other electronic options exchanges. No naked options. Options tickets count toward data discounts but not commission discounts.

Bonds: U.S. Treasuries and zero coupon (U.S. Treasury strips)—$45 up to 50K face value. Over 50K, $45 + .001% of face value. Listed and OTC corporate bonds—$5/bond. Minimum of $35/transaction.

Margin: Brokers call plus .5% to 1.75%; currently 7% to 8¼%.

APPEALING FEATURES: Demo page of Level 1; interactive one-week test drive of Level 4 with $100,000 paper account.

SUPPORT SYSTEMS: Toll-free, priority-client-only phone number. Access to live UltimateTrader chat room for client services. Free Briefing.com.

OPERATIONAL SYSTEMS:

CPU: 300MHz Pentium II processor.

Memory: 96MB RAM.

Hard disk: 3.2 GB with 3.5" 1.44 MB floppy disk drive, CD-ROM drive, mouse, and keyboard.

Operating system: Windows NT 4.0 workstation with service pack pcANYWHERE32 v8.0 client.

Monitor: 17-inch SVGA color. If split monitors are used, Appian, STB, or Color Graphix installation is suggested.

BACKGROUND INFORMATION: A.B. Watley, member NASD/SIPC, a broker/dealer founded in 1958, is a wholly-owned subsidiary of Internet Financial Services, Inc.

ALL-TECH INVESTMENT GROUP, INC.

URL: www.attain.com

TYPE OF SITE: Direct access online and after-hours trading.

USERS: Active day traders.

SNAIL MAIL: 160 Summit Avenue
Montvale, NJ 07645

PHONE: 1-888-3ATTAIN (328-8246)

E-MAIL: trade@attain.com

SERVICES: Nasdaq Level II real-time market data and point-and-click order entry. Market monitoring by customizable analytical programs and tickers. Total trade anonymity.

EXECUTION SYSTEMS: Traders can modify, update, cancel, and refresh their orders with a click through the Attain ECN. Clearing firm is Penson Financial Services, Inc.

FEES:

Account minimum: $25,000 for active day trading; $15,000 for casual trading; $10,000 for retail accounts. $100,000 trading capital recommended.

Software commission: $250/calendar month, waived at 200 transactions per month. Real-time Level II, multiple Nasdaq screens through Data Broadcasting Corp. using Signal Online or StockEdge Online, or ATTAIN® System. ATTAIN execution features interface with either. Fast executions and immediate confirmations.

Trades: Nasdaq—$25/transaction. Listed—$25/transaction plus $.005/share up to 2000 shares. Add $.015 for 2001 shares and above.

ECN fees: ATTN free; $1/ticket for SelectNet. Extra $.015/share for BTRD, REDI, BRUT, and INCA; $1/ticket for ISLD; $.005/share for TNTO. TNTO $.015/share through ECN Direct and BTRD. REDI and BRUT not available.

Pass-through fees: $7.50/transaction for transfer agent; $.01/$300 value on sell side of listed/OTC securities or options for SEC.

Mutual funds: Service fees through Southwest Securities.

IRA accounts: $40/year; $25 setup; closing $60.

Options: $25 + $3/contract.

Treasuries: Bills, $5/trade. Notes and bonds, $15/trade.

APPEALING FEATURES: This site has its own ECN! Exclusive Attain features include "Hit the Street," which allows traders to enter the total number of shares they wish to buy or sell, then enter the number of shares they wish to display to each of the market makers and ECNs showing the best bid or offer. "Hiding Size" allows traders not to display the total quantity wishing to be traded so as to avoid any potential adverse market impact.

SUPPORT SYSTEMS: 1-877-925-5832. Trading demo. Seminars offered through affiliate, All-Tech Training Group (wwww.traintotrade .com). Glossary.

Open account online.

OPERATIONAL SYSTEMS:

CPU: Pentium II 266 MHz (minimum).

Memory: 64MB RAM/SDRAM or PC100 6ns.

Hard disk: 1.6 GIG EIDE HDD plus 1.44 MB 3.5" floppy drive.

Video: 2 MB DRAM (capable of supporting 1280×1024 resolution).

Modem: 28.8 kbps (minimum).

Operating system: Win95/98 or NT 4.0 workstation.

Cache: 256 pipeline burst cache (minimum).

CD-ROM: 8× (minimum).

Monitor: 17-inch .28mm 1280×1024 dpi (minimum) (noninterlaced interface) with Windows 95-compatible keyboard and logitech standard mouse.

Other programs: Norton AntiVirus, PC Anywhere 8.0, fax modem software.

Before plugging in or turning on your terminal, you must have a dedicated telephone line.

BACKGROUND INFORMATION: All-Tech CEO Harvey Houtkin, an advocate of reform of investing rules and regulations in favor of individual investors, is the author of *Secrets of the SOES Bandit.*

ANDOVER TRADING

URL: www.andovertrading.com

TYPE OF SITE: Day trading, including after-hours trading, all markets, limited margin securities.

USERS: Active day traders, primarily in-office. Trading offices in NY, MD, FL, and CO, with many others (e.g, TX, CA, OH) scheduled for opening.

SNAIL MAIL: Andover Trading
30 Broad Street, 39th Floor
New York, NY 10004

PHONE: 1-800-788-2717
1-888-398-ANDV (398-2638)

SERVICES: In-office Pentium processors with Pro 400 and 21-inch monitors. Real-time quote/order entry system from CyberStock.

EXECUTION SYSTEMS: Andover Brokerage executes all orders on an agency basis, and does not make markets in any stocks.

FEES:
  Account minimum: $50,000 recommended to begin trading.
  Trades: Online—$8/trade. Broker-assisted—$18/trade. ECN charges
    additional.
  In-house commissions: OTC—10–20 shares, $20; 21–30 shares, $18;
    31–40 shares, $17; 41–60 shares, $16; 61–80 shares, $15; 81+
    shares, $14. NYSE—1–5,000,000 shares, $10 + $.125/share;
    5,000,001 shares and up, $10 + $.01/share. Instinet—Ticket +
    $1.01/share.

APPEALING FEATURES: After-hours trading via Instinet.

SUPPORT SYSTEMS: Toll-free numbers to live representatives.

OPERATIONAL SYSTEMS: The following configuration is recommended:
  CPU: 300MHz Pentium II.
  Memory: 96MB RAM.

Hard disk: 3.2 GB with 3.5" 1.44 MB floppy disk drive, CD-ROM drive, mouse, and keyboard.

Operating system: Windows NT 4.0 workstation with service pack pcANYWHERE32 v8.0 client.

Monitor: 17-inch SVGA color. If split monitors are used, Appian, STB, or Color Graphix installation is recommended.

BACKGROUND INFORMATION: Andover Trading, member NASD, was started in 1993 and is a division of Andover Brokerage LLC, a broker-dealer with corporate offices in New York.

BROADWAY TRADING LLC

URL: www.broadwaytrading.com

TYPE OF SITE: A broker-dealer specializing in Nasdaq executions by Internet, remote order entry terminal, or in office.

USERS: Professional day traders.

SNAIL MAIL: 50 Broad Street, 2nd Floor
New York, NY 10004

PHONE: 1-212-328-3555

E-MAIL: info@daytrading.com

SERVICES: Offices in New York City, on Long Island, and in Boca Raton, FL. Proprietary trading system, The Watcher, provides instant access to Nasdaq Level II quotes and fast, low-cost executions, as well as the ability to actively follow the market, monitor positions, and account activity, and gain access to Island ECN.

EXECUTION SYSTEMS: After firm approval, all orders are immediately sent to the appropriate market or posted on Island ECN for execution. Clearing company is Datek Online Brokerage Services Corp., member NASD/SIPC.

FEES:
Account minimum: $75,000 (cash and/or marginable securities) to open.
Trades: From $.02 to $.04/share per trade.

APPEALING FEATURES: Watcher download allows for a live demo at home.

SUPPORT SYSTEMS: Hands-on training on use of Watcher. Support available by e-mail: support@broadwaytrading.com. Navigational overview and chat room. Link to Tradersedge.net—independent source for books, videos, training CD, and 5-day seminar. Link to day trading educational products from independent Broadway Consulting Group: www.electronicdaytrader.com or 1-212-378-4000.

Open an account by calling a Broadway Trading registered rep at 1-212-328-3555.

OPERATIONAL SYSTEMS: Telephone service options for remote traders only:

Direct dial-up or Winstar contract (800 or 888 number): $850 deposit ($750 refundable upon closing account), includes $100 for line setup fee. $.08/minute; $250 minimum per month.

Hardware requirements for remote traders:

CPU: IBM-compatible, Pentium-based with color monitor.

Modem: U.S. Robotics (3COM).

BACKGROUND INFORMATION: Broadway Trading LLC, member NASD/SIPC, is a broker-dealer founded by Marc Friedfertig, member of NYSE and co-author of *The Electronic Day Trader* and *Electronic Day Traders' Secrets*.

CYBER BROKER INC.

URL: www.cybercorp.com

TYPE OF SITE: Full-service brokerage offering Level II and direct access online trading.

USERS: Active online investors and day traders.

SNAIL MAIL: 1601 Rio Grande, Suite 456
              Austin, TX 78701

PHONE: 1-512-3220-5444

E-MAIL: online icon.

SERVICES: Three account styles. Trading rooms. Charting and technical analysis. Daily research available from DLJ and Wall Street Whispers. NewsClient in development for monitoring all market activity/news.

EXECUTION SYSTEMS: Trading through CyBerXchange, a proprietary intelligent Central Order Routing and Execution (CORE) system allowing traders to interact with Market Makers and ECNs. Clearing firm is Penson Financial Services, Inc.

FEES:

CyBerTrader/CyBerT Account: $250/month for up to 99 tickets per month; free with 100 or more tickets per month (real-time, Level II data). $15,000 initial trading capital to open, maintain daily equity balance of $7500; minimum annual income of $50,000; net worth of $100,000 exclusive of home; and experience using an online broker.

CyBerX Account: $49/month for up to 50 tickets per month; free with 51 or more tickets per month (real-time, dynamic Level I data). $10,000 initial trading capital to open, maintain daily equity balance of $5000; minimum annual income of $35,000; net worth of $65,000 exclusive of home; and experience using an online broker.

Trades: $19.95/ticket for up to 199 tickets per month. $18.95/ticket for 200–299 tickets per month. $17.95/ticket for 300–399 tickets per month. $16.95/ticket for 400–499 tickets per month. $15.95/ticket for 500–599 tickets per month. $14.95/ticket for 600 or more tickets per month.

No maximum ticket size; however, maximum order size is 20,000 shares.

No additional base fee for multiple fills within 5 minutes of initial execution.

Additional processing fees may apply to tickets of $1000 and over.

An SEC charge of $.000033/share for all sell orders executed by CyBerBroker is added to total commission fee.

ECN fees: SOES and Island Direct are free. No cancel fees. Add $1/trade for SNET Direct or Attain Direct; $2.50/trade for SNET Broadcast; $.0025/share for ISLD, REDI; $.015/share for BRUT, INCA; $.005/share for ATTN, BTRD, TNTO, NYSE.

APPEALING FEATURES: Demos of both levels of data service/trading. Free software download.

SUPPORT SYSTEMS: Hot lines include 1-512-320-8930 for technical assistance; 1-512-320-0833 for trading assistance; 1-512-320-5444 for training assistance. Online chat system, training CD, manuals. Data visualization and decision support.

OPERATIONAL SYSTEMS: Standard upgrade.

BACKGROUND INFORMATION: CyBer Broker is a wholly-owned subsidiary of CyBerCorp, formed in 1995.

DELTA TRADER

URL: www.deltatrader.com

TYPE OF SITE: Day trading firm with after-hours trading and IPO offerings.

USERS: Active day traders.

SNAIL MAIL: 220 Montgomery Street, Suite 777
San Francisco, CA 94104

PHONE: 1-888-781-0283

SERVICES: Before-and-after market hours trading via Instinet, available through investment representative only (1-800-877-3311). Delta Trader is a browser-based, online trading service; and Delta Trader PRO is a software-based electronic execution system for day traders. Real-time snap quotes, delayed stock and option matrix, and intraday portfolio updates.

EXECUTION SYSTEMS: All securities offered through Preferred Capital. Electronic execution of stocks (option orders via RAES, POETS, AMOS, or AUTOM systems).

FEES:

Account minimum: $1000 for Delta Trader; $5000 for Delta Trader PRO. Comprehensive data feed subscription available. ECN fees are passed through.

Trades: OTC—$7.75/trade. Listed—$.02/share for market orders; $.03/share for limit orders. Minimum $15/trade.

Options: Under $10, $2.50/contract; over $10, $3/contract. Minimum $19.95/trade.

Mutual funds: $15–$30.

IRA accounts: $25 setup, $45 annual, $100 closing.

Bonds: $35 minimum.

Treasuries: $35/order.

Rates for one-on-one relationships with a Preferred Investment Representative are negotiated. For more information, call 1-800-877-3311.

APPEALING FEATURES: After-hours trading.

SUPPORT SYSTEMS: Toll-free number. Extensive research. Order entry demo; software tutorial.

Download forms or e-mail request to open account.

OPERATIONAL SYSTEMS: Standard with Netscape Navigator (version 3.0 or higher) or Microsoft Internet Explorer (version 3.0 or higher).

BACKGROUND INFORMATION: Delta Trader (formerly Active Investor) is a division of Preferred Capital Markets, Inc.

DLJ DIRECT INC.

URL: www.DLJdirect.com

TYPE OF SITE: Level II trading as well as after-hours trading and on-line IPO offerings.

USERS: Day traders.

SNAIL MAIL: 4211 S. 102nd Street
Omaha, NE 68103-2227

PHONE: 1-877-355-5557

E-MAIL: service@dljdirect.com

SERVICES: After-hours trading available exclusively to Select Clients. Call 1-877-355-5678 for information about additional benefits and privileges. Proprietary MarketSpeed software accesses all features of site, including customizable investing tools. ALERT! provides online and e-mail notification for price changes and account information. Real-time online order execution reports. AssetMaster integrates account with 120 days of transaction history.

FEES:

Account minimum: None. No monthly maintenance fee. Select Clients must maintain at least $1,000,000 assets in combined DLJdirect accounts.

Quotes: Delayed quotes and info available on log-in; real-time quotes available on log-in during market hours. 100 free real-time quotes on account activation; 100 additional quotes with each executed trade.

Trades: $20/trade up to 1000 shares + $.02/share thereafter.

Broker-assisted: 1-800-825-5873. No commission for bonds, precious metals, or Treasuries not bought at auction.

Penny stocks: Minimum $20 to a maximum of 5% of principal per trade.

Mutual funds: $35 for no-load/low-load funds; $20 for exchange between funds; $5000 investment minimum ($1000 for retirement account).

Options: $40/transaction up to $2500; $80/transaction of $2501–$5000; $220/transaction of $5001–$10,000; $480 + .003% of principal for transactions of $10,001+. Maximum charge of $35/contract on first 2 contracts, $4/contract thereafter. Minimum charge of $35 + $1.75/contract. Overriding minimum ticket charge $40.

Margin: 7%, plus sliding scale from +1.5% down to −.5%, based on increasing average margin balance.

APPEALING FEATURES: Upon activation of new account, free 60-day trial to participate in online IPOs and to receive Standard & Poor's, Reuters, NYTimes, Business Wire, PR NewsWire, TheStreet.com, Lipper, Zacks, Briefing.com, and DLJ's proprietary analysts' research. Minimum asset balance of $100,000 required to continue without charge.

SUPPORT SYSTEMS: E-mail and 24-hour customer support (1-800-825-5723). Portfolio and trade demos. Stock Center and FundCenter® are used to search stocks and funds according to custom criteria.

OPERATIONAL SYSTEMS: Standard. Available across all platforms.

BACKGROUND INFORMATION: Originally launched as PC Financial Network®, DLJdirect is currently the only online brokerage offering Donaldson, Lufkin & Jenrette research and IPOs to the online, self-directed investor.

EDGETRADE SECURITIES LLC

URL: www.edgetrade.com

TYPE OF SITE: Full service brokerage firm capable of Level II and after-hours trading.

USERS: Day traders.

SNAIL MAIL: 5 Hanover Square, 10th Floor
New York, NY 10004

PHONE: 1-888-440-EDGE (440-3343)

E-MAIL: info@edgetrade.com

SERVICES: Real-time inside (bid, offer, volume, size) quotes for Nasdaq Level II and NYSE. Access to execution system, live confirmations, real-time futures, time of sales, new high/low tickers. Technical data and graphics analysis, index indicators, price change alerts, and other features.

EXECUTION SYSTEMS: Trader-directed executions on SOES, Island, SelectNet, Island/ECNs, SuperDOT, and Instinet.

FEES:
Account minimum: $25,000; $50,000–$100,000 trading capital recommended.

Data fees: $280/month for TradeCast plus exchange fees of $58.50/month. Both are free with trading over 150,000 shares per month.

Trades: $.055/share for up to 3999 shares per day; $.035/share for 4000–9999, $.025/share for 10,000–19,999, and $.02/share for 20,000+ shares per day. Additional price breaks for higher-volume traders.

ECN fees: $.015/share for BRUT, INCA; $.01/share for NYSE/AMEX (DOT); and $.005/share for ATTN, BTRD, TNTO, REDI.

APPEALING FEATURES: Training program for electronic day trading (3-week in-house workshop) for $2500.

SUPPORT SYSTEMS: EDGESupport—live help online during market hours, plus toll-free number and e-mail. EDGEBoard—trader bulletin board. EDGEChat—trader chat room. Glossary. Dow Jones and Reuters news available with data feed.

OPERATIONAL SYSTEMS: Standard upgrade.

BACKGROUND INFORMATION: EDGETrade Securities LLC is a member NASD/SIPC.

THE EXECUTIONER LLC

URL: www.executioner.com

TYPE OF SITE: Day trading firm offering Level II point-and-click order entry and after-hours trading.

USERS: Active day traders.

SNAIL MAIL: 7-11 Broadway, Suite 217
White Plains, NY 10601

PHONE: 1-877-453-8352

E-MAIL: staff@executioner.com

SERVICES: Two account levels to choose from. Executioner I (for single screen users) includes Level II screen, real-time chart display, interest list (unlimited stock groups), stock tickers, position manager, stock monitor, and audible alarms. Executioner II (for multiple screen users) offers unlimited creation of Nasdaq Level II screens.

EXECUTION SYSTEMS: All transactions executed via Terra Nova Trading LLC. Clearing firm is Southwest Securities, Inc.

FEES:

Account minimum: $10,000.

Executioner I: $175/month for RealTick III, plus $58.50/month for exchange fees. Refundable after 25 transactions per month. $22.50/trade. Unlimited ticket size for Nasdaq and up to 2000 shares for listed; add $.01/share over 2000.

Executioner II: $250/month for RealTick III, plus $58.50/month for exchange fees. Refundable after 50 transactions per month. $22.50/trade up to 19 trades per month; $21.95/trade for 20–49, $20.95/trade for 50–99, $19.95/trade for 100–149, and $18.95/trade for 150+ trades per month. Unlimited ticket size for Nasdaq and up to 2000 shares for listed; add $.01/share over 2000.

Options: $25 minimum per ticket; $3–$7/option. Exchange fees $55–$60/month.

ECN fees: Added to all applicable trades.

Data fees: Dow Jones news, $95/month. COMTEX real-time news,

$50/mo. Special offer of discount subscriptions to Pristine Day Trader Real Time Trading Room, Real-Time Idea Machine, and LiveWire.

APPEALING FEATURES: Toll-free numbers for new accounts (1-877-453-8352), technical support (1-888-843-9286), and trading desk (1-877-843-9999). Urgent trades only: 1-877-967-5488.

SUPPORT SYSTEMS: Toll-free number and e-mail. Glossary. Demo. In-house seminar. Instruction manual for downloading. Self-executing movies/tutorials. Margin tutorial. Chat room. Extensive links to research.

OPERATIONAL SYSTEMS: Standard upgrade with multiple monitors.

BACKGROUND INFORMATION: The Executioner LLC is a branch office of Terra Nova Trading LLC.

INSIDER TRADING

URL: www.insider-trading.net

TYPE OF SITE: Online brokerage firm with execution direction capabilities.

USERS: All levels of online traders; check for registration in your state.

SNAIL MAIL: Investor Relations
PanAmerican BanCorp
300 Wheeler Road, Suite 108
Hauppauge, NY 11788

PHONE: 1-516-951-1638

E-MAIL: customersvcs@insider-trading.net

SERVICES: Real-time quotes, Level II market maker and exchange data, news, charts, historical data, time and sales data, portfolio management, tickers, real-time buying power.

EXECUTION SYSTEMS: Investors are able to execute trades on the Nasdaq, NYSE, and AMEX directly and execute buy/sell orders of mutual funds and fixed-income securities via Insider Trading's Customer Service Center. Clearing company is Gold Country Securities, Inc.

FEES:
Account minimum: $5000, of which $1000 must be in cash.
Trades: Rates begin at $21.95. There is a $10 extra fee per call-in trade. Exchanges or ECNs may add additional fees: ARCA—$2.75/trade; ATTN—$.015/share; Bloomberg—$.015/share; Instinet—$.0075/share; Island—$.0025/share; Listed—$.01/share; REDI—$.015/share; SOES—$.50/trade (1000 shares or less on Nasdaq) with cancels at $.25/occurrence.
BB: $30/order for up to 50,000 shares.
Mutual funds: $40–$80, based on principal amount of no-load funds.
IRA accounts: $50 annual, $50 closing.
Margin: 8.75%.

SUPPORT SYSTEMS: 9 am–7 pm EST through America Online's Instant Messenger Program.

OPERATIONAL SYSTEMS: Windows 95 or Windows NT, Pentium-based processor (75 MHz minimum) with a minimum of 16 MB RAM (32 MB recommended); 28.8 kbps or faster modem (56 kbps recommended); 28.8 kbps or faster Internet connection with unlimited access.

BACKGROUND INFORMATION: Insider Trading, member NASD/SIPC, is a service of Gold Country Securities, Inc. and PanAmerican BanCorp.

JPR CAPITAL—NET TRADER

URL: www.jprcapital.com

TYPE OF SITE: Day trading site with streaming real-time Level II data and order entry, plus after-hours trading. No options, futures, or penny stock trading.

USERS: Day traders. Canadian residents accepted.

SNAIL MAIL: One World Trade Center
Suite 8735
New York, NY 10048

PHONE: 1-212-938-2305
1-800-JPR-2004 (577-2004)

E-MAIL: info@jprcapital.com

SERVICES: Dynamically updated real-time trading and portfolio management program using Townsend Analytics RealTick III with data from S&P Comstock. In-branch office trading (2 offices in NY, 1 in NJ), with Insight trading software, at a trading desk with 4 to 8 other traders. Daily market comment with current highlights. Daily short list.

EXECUTION SYSTEMS: Nasdaq trading on SOES—up to 1000 shares per ticket. Uses SelectNet and a "third market" (for same access as institutions) to execute between bid and ask. Handles after-hours trading, and as a member of Island ECN, can bid or offer stock at, between, or away from the market. Listed market, limit, or stop orders are executed on DOT or CSS. All transactions are cleared through Southwest Securities, Inc., a NYSE-listed company.

FEES:

Account minimum: $10,000. All data, exchange, and software fees are waived with 400 or more tickets per month.

Data fees: S&P Comstock, $250/month. Subscription to Real Audio (first 2 weeks free), $200/month.

Trades: Nasdaq—$10/ticket up to 2000 shares, plus ECN fees. Listed market, limit, stop trades—$10/ticket up to 2000 shares, plus $.015/share over 2000.

Exchange fees: AMEX, $4.25/month; NYSE, $5.25/month; Nasdaq Level II, $50/month.

ECN fees: SOES, $.50/ticket; Island, $1/ticket; SelectNet, $2.50/ticket; ARCA, $.01/share + any pass-through routing charges by Select-Net, Island, BTrade, BRUT, REDI, Instinet, or other destinations.

APPEALING FEATURES: "Real Audio"—Daily broadcast of JPR Capital's trading room morning meeting (8:45 am EST) provides trading strategy and tactics, specific stocks to watch or avoid, and insights on market conditions. JPR president announces all his trades as he enters them. Includes training sessions at 1 pm EST, Tuesdays and Thursdays, where traders can ask questions about specific trades and technical analysis, correct entry and exit points, and correct indications for going short or long. JPR is adding a T1 line exclusively for this feature. Download Real Audio player from site.

SUPPORT SYSTEMS: Daily technical and trading support. Link to books (Amazon.com). Free 8-week training course for novices to experienced traders includes market maker and stock symbols, industry groups, technical and fundamental analysis, software, hardware, and trading strategies. Trading demo and FAQs.

Open an account by e-mailing online application, or download application and fax it, or call toll-free number. JPR will mail you S&P forms. You will be given a user ID and password within 2 business days after the completed S&P forms, and your check or wire for minimum of $10,000, are received.

OPERATIONAL SYSTEMS:
CPU: Pentium II or higher.
Memory: 64MB RAM/SDRAM or PC100 6ns.
Hard disk: 2GB or higher.
Video: 4MB PCI video card (any brand).
Modem: Minimum 56k v.90 with cable connection (there is also DSL and ISDN).
Operating system: Win95/98 or NT 4.0 workstation with sound card and speakers.

BACKGROUND INFORMATION: JPR Capital, member NASD/SIPC, was founded in 1995 by President Paul Umansky, a 12-year Wall Street veteran, and his partner Jeffrey Wolf.

MB TRADING INC.

URL: www.mbtrading.com

TYPE OF SITE: Agency order entry firm for all listed/OTC U.S. equities plus options and futures. Does not sell order flow. Before-and-after market hours trading through phone-in order desk and Instinet. No hedge accounts or BB trades permitted.

USERS: Online traders and investors. Professionals may not use SOES and have additional fees.

SNAIL MAIL: 840 Apollo Street, Suite 251
El Segundo, CA 90245

PHONE: 1-310-414-9299
1-888-790-4800

E-MAIL: clients@mbtrading.com

SERVICES: Three levels of data configurations (MB Trader, MB Custom, MB Lite) with dynamically updated real-time trading and portfolio management program using RealTick III and Level II data.

EXECUTION SYSTEMS: All trades are executed by Terra Nova Trading LLC, a registered broker-dealer, through ARCA, ISLD, INCA, SelectNet, SOES, and SuperDOT for the NYSE and AMEX markets, and access to ATTN, BTRD, and REDI ECNs. All transactions are cleared through Southwest Securities, Inc., a NYSE-listed company.

FEES:

Account minimum: $5000 equity to open margin account; minimum equity of $2000.

MB Trader: Fully customizable, fully featured trading software for Internet-based order entry with streaming real-time Level II quotes. $300/month for 1–19 trades; $100/month for 20–49 trades. No charge with 50+ trades per month. ($300 deposit refundable when account is closed.)

MB Custom: Single, fixed-page Level II quotes and limited charting. $200/month for 1–19 trades. No charge with 20+ trades per month. ($200 deposit refundable when account is closed.)

MB Lite: Real-time Level I quotes, full order entry module.

$115/month for 1–19 trades. No charge with 20+ trades per month. Add $50/month for Nasdaq Level II data feed. ($115 deposit refundable when account is closed.)

Data fees: Dow Jones Online News, $95/month; News Watch, $75/month (with Zacks for $15/month extra); Sort Wizard, $30/month or free with 30 trades per month.

Trades: $22.95/trade for 1–19 trades per month; $21.95/trade for 20–49, $19.95/trade for 40–99, $17.95/trade for 100–199, $16.95/trade for 200–399, and $14.95/trade for 400+ trades per month. Add $.01/share over 2000 for any listed issues. No additional charge for quotes given via telephone or for phoned-in trades executed by reps.

A trade equals one buy or sell ticket. A single ticket is 10,000 shares (or less) on Nasdaq, or 2000 shares (or less) on listed securities. A single trade/order/ticket generates only one commission regardless of partial or multiple fills.

ECN/exchange fees: $65 futures exchange fee (optional); waived after 50 trades per month. All other exchange fees are included. Add $.015/share for Instinet trades. All other ECNs, no charge.

Options: $20 minimum ticket. 1–5 lot size, $7/option; 6–20 lot size, $4/option; 21+ lot size, $3/option. No minimum balance required.

IRA accounts: No setup or annual fee, $25 closing.

APPEALING FEATURES: Low-cost options trading; before-and-after market hours trading.

SUPPORT SYSTEMS: 24-hour daily telephone support. Instructional tutorials in day trading order entry techniques at no extra cost. Software demos. Live chat room. FAQs included on site.

Open account by downloading, completing, and mailing forms. Notification by e-mail by the end of the second business day (from receipt) with complete instructions on obtaining and installing the software, funding the account, and setting up to begin learning the software.

OPERATIONAL SYSTEMS: MB Trader requires 32-bit operation.
CPU: Pentium-based with minimum 200 MHz processor.
Memory: 64MB RAM.

Hard disk: 20 MB minimum (2GB or even 4GB recommended).

Modem: 56k analog Internet connection and ISDN. (Cable modem, DSL, and ADSL acceptable.)

Operating system: Win95/98 with 2MB video card.

Hookup: Use a major ISP and a backup (secondary) ISP. UUNET, the country's largest ISP, offers a VPN (virtual private network) alternative.

BACKGROUND INFORMATION: MB Trading Inc. is a division of Terra Nova Trading LLC, member NASD/SIPC.

ON-SITE TRADING, INC.

URL: www.onsitetrading.com

TYPE OF SITE: Full service discount brokerage capable of Level II trading on the Internet, via personal dedicated frame-relay phone line, or onsite at branch offices. Does not sell order flow or act as a principal. Before-and-after market hours trading via Instinet.

USERS: Very active day traders. Proprietary traders (trading with the firm's capital) use the Great Neck main office. There are also 9 branch offices (4 in NY, 3 in FL, 1 in MD, 1 in NJ) for private customers as well as remote trading.

SNAIL MAIL: 98 Cutter Mill Road, Suite 100
Great Neck, NY 11021

PHONE: 1-516-482-9292
1-888-402-0533

E-MAIL: mikem@onsitetrading.com

SERVICES: In-branch office trading with quote/charting software: S&P Comstock, Bloomberg, Bridge Financial, Bristol Insight, Redi Plus, Track Data, and TradeCast. News services include Bloomberg, Bridge, Dow Jones, First Call, and Reuters. Trading on NYSE, AMEX, Nasdaq, Nasdaq II, SOES, SelectNet, and all ECNs.

EXECUTION SYSTEMS: Trades are placed on the primary exchange market or ECN specified by the trader. Spear, Leeds & Kellogg, one of the largest and most established U.S. clearing firms, is the clearing agent.

FEES:

Account minimum: $25,000. Annual income must be at least $50,000, and net worth at least $150,000. Margin accounts available.

Basic service: $100/month; waived for 40+ trades per month. S&P dynamic real-time quotes and nonpro exchange fees for NYSE, AMEX, Nasdaq, and Nasdaq II. Rapid executions and immediate confirmations for NYSE, AMEX, Instinet, SOES, SelectNet, and ECNs.

Advanced service: $300/month; waived for 100+ trades per month. S&P dynamic real-time quotes and nonpro exchange fees for

NYSE, AMEX, Nasdaq, Nasdaq II, CME, CBT, and OPRA/options. Rapid executions and immediate confirmations for NYSE, AMEX, Instinet, SOES, SelectNet and ECNs. Dynamic real-time charts and technical studies, and Dow Jones news service.

Nasdaq trades: $19.95/trade for 1–250 trades per month; $18.95/trade for 251–500, $17.95/trade for 501–1000, and $16.95/trade for 1001–1500 trades per month. Commissions negotiable for over 1500 trades. ECNs charges additional, if used.

Listed trades: NYSE/AMEX, $14.95 + $.01/share per trade for 1–250 trades per month; $13.95 + .01/share per trade for 251–500, $12.95 + $.01/share per trade for 501–1000, and $11.95 + $.01/share per trade for 1001–1500 trades per month. Commissions negotiable for over 1500 trades.

ECN fees: No additional charges for canceled, SOES, or SelectNet orders. ATTN, TNTO, and BTRD (minimum $1.50/trade), $.005/share; ISLD, REDI, $1/trade; INCA, $.015/share.

IRA accounts: $65 setup.

APPEALING FEATURES: Trader can apply for position as proprietary trader. Active trader can negotiate commissions and fees and additional day trading buying power, rather than the standard 2-to-1 margin.

SUPPORT SYSTEMS: Training and help desk. Test drive. Screen shots of various software features and "simulator mode" to walk user through the software. Training manual with software package and NY-office training sessions on using the trading station. Also, one-on-one training sessions by phone and directly through the trading station to make sure users are familiar with all order handling rules and software functions. Trainers can be reached before, during, and after market hours (7:30 am–6 pm EST). Every client has an assigned trader support representative (TSR). Links to various investing magazines. Glossary Side menu bar and site map for easy navigation.

Open an account by downloading, completing, and mailing application and signature forms. After you receive approval notification by phone, arrange a software installation appointment. Use trading simulator for a day to familiarize yourself with software and avoid costly mistrades.

OPERATIONAL SYSTEMS:

CPU: 300MHz Pentium II.

Memory: 96MB RAM.

Hard disk: 3.2 GB with 3.5" 1.44 MB floppy disk drive, CD-ROM drive, mouse, and keyboard.

Operating system: Windows NT 4.0 workstation with service pack pcANYWHERE32 v8.0 client.

Monitor: 17-inch SVGA color. With split monitors, Appian, STB, or Color Graphix installation is recommended.

Hookup: Either frame relay through WorldCom/MCI directly into firm's servers or the fastest service that can guarantee a minimum 50KB connection with little downtime and that supports Windows NT.

BACKGROUND INFORMATION: On-Site Trading, Inc., member NASD/SIPC, was formed in 1994 to provide stock trading services targeted to both the on-premises and remote trader.

SUNLOGIC SECURITIES, INC.

URL: www.sunlogic.com

TYPE OF SITE: Discount brokerage with online trading.

USERS: Active traders. Available only in AZ, CA, GA, MI, NV, NY, VA, and WA.

SNAIL MAIL: 5333 Thornton Avenue
Newark, CA 94560

PHONE: 1-800-556-4600

E-MAIL: online icon.

SERVICES: After-hours trading. Limited to 30 minutes prior to Nasdaq open and up to 45 minutes after NYSE close. Free real-time quotes, symbol search, historical prices, upgrades/downgrades. Portfolio page allows order entry and trade status on same screen. Electronic confirmation. Offers IPOs. Site also in Chinese language.

EXECUTION SYSTEMS: Clearing agent is JBOC.

FEES:
Account minimum: $2000.
Limit trades: $.01/share for Nasdaq; $.02/share for listed stock; minimum trade $32.
Market trades: $15.99 for Nasdaq, + $.02/share for listed stock.
After-hours: SelectNet executions, $40 commission + $3 postage charge.
Broker-assisted: $.02/share; minimum trade $32.
Options: $18 + 1.6% of principal for trades up to $2000; $39 + .7% of principal for trades of $2001–$10,000; $76 + .03% of principal for trades over $10,000.

APPEALING FEATURES: Briefing. Live video from AMEX trading floor. 24-hour news from NPR.

SUPPORT SYSTEMS: Toll-free number. Glossary. Trade demo. Sunlogic research. Bloomberg market report.

OPERATIONAL SYSTEMS: Standard.

BACKGROUND INFORMATION: Sunlogic Securities is a member of NASD/SIPC.

Specialty Sites

The following sites are notable for their specialties—not necessarily to the exclusion of equity trading. Many of the sites listed elsewhere may offer some of the same capabilities, but these sites have brought their concentrated area of expertise online. They include professional trading firms, foreign exchanges, and bonds, mutual funds, and commodities online.

PROFESSIONAL TRADING FIRMS

Designed by traders for traders, professional trading sites provide the technological "back room" advantage for the independent trader or broker. Most require *onsite* trading, touting the benefits of collaborating with other traders—shared ideas, concepts, and motivation. All provide state-of-the-art, multiple screen systems with high-speed order entry and execution, and lower transaction costs thanks to economies of scale. While they're geared toward the full-time trading professional, many professional trading firms also provide extensive training courses, and some accept retail clients.

BRIGHT TRADING, INC.

URL: www.stocktrading.com

PHONE: 1-800-249-7488

Established in 1992 by Robert Bright and Edward Franco, Bright Trading requires a $25,000 deposit to begin trading through one of its 22 sites. Each site can accommodate 12 to 30 people. Branches currently exist in AZ, CO, FL, IL, MA, MD, MI, NV, NY, OH, TN, and WA with new locations planned. No retail clients.

FIELD LOGAN & CO LLC

URL: www.fieldlogan.com

PHONE: 1-888-353-4353

E-MAIL: inquiry@fieldlogan.com

Founded by John Rende, California-based Field Logan is a broker-dealer that offers independent professionals direct access order entry through Automated Financial Systems. Herzog Heine Geduld Inc. provides execution and clearing.

GLOBALINK FINANCIAL NETWORK

URL: www.globalinkusa.com

PHONE: 1-800-388-9788

GlobaLink is a broker-dealer for retail clients as well as independent professionals. Online workstations provide the trading platform and back office support to manage a book on the Internet. Herzog Heine Geduld Inc. provides execution and clearing.

HARBOR SECURITIES

URL: www.harborsecurities.com

PHONE: 1-212-825-9700

Founded by Warren Sulmasy, Harbor uses proprietary TradeNet as a trading platform. Order execution is through MXEdge; clearing through Spear, Leeds & Kellogg. No retail clients.

INTERACTIVE BROKERS, LLC

URL: www.timberhill.com

PHONE: 1-203-618-5710

Interactive Brokers is a division of Timber Hill Group, formed in 1977 by computer programmer Thomas Peterffy. Interactive provides screen-based trading with online execution services in listed equity and equity-based derivatives in the United States and Europe. Depending on the product, traders have instant access to a specialist book, a trading pit, or an electronic exchange. The site is available to professionals as well as retail clients residing in the United States, United Kingdom, Germany, Switzerland, France, and Hong Kong.

LA SALLE ST. TRADING LLC

URL: www.lasalletrading.com

PHONE: 1-312-705-3049
Formed in 1997 as a division of LaSalle St. Securities, Inc., La Salle St. Trading is affiliated with introducing broker Momentum Securities. Clearing is done through Southwest Securities. La Salle has trading rooms in Chicago and Milwaukee to provide novices as well as professionals with a facility for electronic day trading. Offers $2,000 3-week training course.

SUNSTATE EQUITY TRADING, INC.

URL: www.sunstateequitytrading.com

PHONE: 1-813-961-4649
A Tampa, Florida, based broker/dealer, member NASD/SIPC, Sunstate offers day trading to remote access Internet clients via modem or digital line (recommends Time-Warners Road Runner coaxial cable). Requires $10,000 account minimum (compared to $50,000 for onsite traders). Clearing agent is Penson Financial Services.

VAN BUREN SECURITIES, LLC

URL: www.vbsecurities.com

PHONE: 1-888-781-9400
Van Buren offers multiple physical locations for professional electronic trading as well as remote dial-up access. No retail clients.

FOREIGN SECURITIES

Individual trading in other countries is not yet as prolific as it is in the United States; however, the market is building rapidly. Most of the sites in this small group allow U.S. clients to buy foreign securities in foreign currency, and offer U.S. products as well.

Australia

COMMONWEALTH SECURITIES LIMITED

URL: www.comsec.com

PHONE: 61-2-9206-5400
Exclusively Australian Stock Exchange; all payments in Australian currency. Clearing through CHESS (Clearing House Electronic Subregister System). No account minimum noted. $29/Internet trade; $50/broker-assisted trade.

STOCK ROCKET

URL: www.stockrocket.com

PHONE: 1-800-653-835
02-9241-4800

E-MAIL: admin@stockrocket.com.au
No establishment fees to open a share trading account. The usual fee on share transactions is 1.5% (minimum US$75 per contract). For Australian shares the flat rate is $49 up to $10,000; $75 for $10,000–$75,000; 0.1% above $75,000. First trade is only $24.50 on market ASX-listed securities up to $100,000. Clearing is through Bear Stearns Securities Corporation (U.S.).

Free Web site access for regular traders who place a minimum of 4 trades per month. Less frequent traders pay only the fees and royalties charged by the Australian Stock Exchange and the information service provider Equityworld. For regular investors, $16.50 per month includes 3000 real-time quotes (as 300 pages of 10 quotes maximum) and 30 ASX announcements per month.

Argentina

PATAGON.COMARGENTINA

URL: www.patagon.com

PHONE: 5411-4343-7270

E-MAIL: support@patagon.com

Patagon.com is the first service in Latin America to offer Internet trading facilities for local securities. Patagon.com currently provides this service through InvestCapital S.A., a licensed securities dealer regulated by the Mercado de Valores de Buenos Aires and the Comision Nacional de Valores. Cash is held on account by Patagon.com at Citibank, N.A., 111 Wall Street, New York, NY 10043. Patagon.com will soon be providing trading facilities through registered broker-dealers in the Brazilian, Mexican, and Chilean markets, and is positioning itself to be a regional transaction hub that will allow clients to invest transparently in any Latin American market.

There is no minimum amount to open an account. The custody fee is US$2 month (if you have stocks in your account). For each buy or sell of equities, the commission is 0.5% plus market tax of .0951%; for bonds, 0.5% plus tax of 0.02%; and for options, 1% plus tax of 0.2%. The minimum commission in all cases is US$10.

Belize

BHI SECURITIES

URL: www.bhisecurities.com

PHONE: 501-2-72390

E-MAIL: mmoreno@btl.net

Not open to U.S. or Belize residents. BHI Securities is a subsidiary of BHI Corporation (BHI) and an affiliate of the Belize Bank Limited (the Belize Bank), Belize's largest bank. Investors throughout the world with Internet access can trade in complete privacy in U.S. securities. Clearing is through U.S. Clearing Corp.

There is a one-time fee of $1500 to establish a corporation. This fee includes the services of a corporate director who will open both a corporate bank account and a corporate Internet trading account with the firm Thomas F. White & Co., Inc. of San Francisco. After your account is established, all funds are allocated between your corporate bank and trading accounts. In subsequent years, an annual fee of $500 is charged to maintain your corporation's legal status.

The opening account minimum is $10,000. Trading accounts must maintain minimum asset values of $25,000. The commission on equities is $39/trade and $.02/share; options, $39/trade and $2.50/contract. All executions are subject to a $2.50 processing charge.

Canada

GREEN LINE INVESTOR SERVICES INC.

URL: www.greenline.ca

PHONE: 1-800-667-6299

E-MAIL: edshelp@tdbank.ca
For Canadian customers only—no U.S. or Australian residents—to trade on all Canadian and U.S. exchanges.

Green Line Investor Services is a division of TD Securities Inc. (TD Bank). It offers trading through WebBroker (Internet trading site), MicroMax (DOS and Macintosh trading software), and TeleMax (touch-tone phone trading system). In addition, there is a full range of online banking services and TalkBroker, a speech recognition service that lets you access quotes from any telephone. Flat fee-based pricing is in Canadian dollars.

New Zealand

DFMTRADE

URL: www.dfmainland.co.nz/

PHONE: 011-64-9-307-9066

D.F. Mainland Group Limited is an independent, privately owned financial services company, originally established in 1951, that began online trading operations in 1996. The group is now equipped to service institutions, midsize corporations, and private investors in trading of securities listed on the New Zealand Stock Exchange (NZSE), as well as in U.S. and U.K. markets. There is no charge for the client software, and the brokerage rate is currently 1% for all transactions, with a minimum brokerage of NZ$30 per transaction. A minimum deposit of NZ$1000 is required.

Hong Kong

BOOM SECURITIES LIMITED

URL: www.boomhq.com

PHONE: 1-852-2123-1000

Established in March 1997 as Asia's first internet broker, trades exclusively listed Hong Kong Stock Exchange in Hong Kong currency in association with Hong Kong Shanghai Banking Corporation Ltd. Features Virtual Dealing Room and Boom-mail internal messaging system. Offers *Cyber Stock Challenge*—first real-time internet Hong Kong stock trading game.

MANSION HOUSE GROUP LIMITED

URL: www.mansionhse.com

PHONE: 011-852-2843-1431

Formed in 1982, Mansion House is an independent investment firm providing financial services to corporations, financial institutions, and individual investors, including stock brokerage services for the Hong Kong Stock Exchange as well as overseas exchanges. It also trades Hang Seng Index futures, precious metals, and commodities.

Trading costs (in HK dollars for securities listed on the Hong Kong exchange) depend on the size of the transaction, but are never less than .25% of the consideration, with a minimum charge of HK$150. Share margin credit facilities are available to approved local clients on selected active stocks. Users need to sign up with outside companies for real-time quotes. Following are some providers of HK quotes:

Netvigator Financial Express (http://nfx.netvigator.com)
  HK$428/month
QuotePower (http://www.quotepower.com) HK$550/month
AsiaNetVest (http://www.AsiaNetVest.com) HK$380/month
AsianUpdate (http://www.asianupdate.com)HK$428/month

Singapore

PHILLIP GNI FUTURES PTE LTD.

URL: www.phillipfutures.com

PHONE: 011-65-538-0500
Phillip GNI Futures offers 24-hour execution and clearing services for institutions and individual investors at SIMEX floor teams in Singapore.

BONDS

Bonds, unlike stocks, can't all be purchased online. Most individual bonds trade over the counter, meaning that publicly available price data is scarce. Many securities trading sites claim to offer bonds, but provide only inventory and pricing information online and require that orders be placed by phone—adding to potential costs. E*Trade, Discover Brokerage, and others do offer online bond purchasing with real-time prices in addition to their securities trading. If bonds are your thing, look for sites that offer large bond inventories, real-time prices, and on-the-spot ordering. You may also want to check out the following.

BONDAGENT LLC

URL: www.taxfreebond.com

PHONE: 1-800-803-9052
The first online brokerage devoted exclusively to the bond market. Affiliated with Vanguard Capital and BT Alex Brown. Includes comprehensive research.

U.S. TREASURY DEPARTMENT— "BUREAU OF PUBLIC DEBT ONLINE"

URL: www.publicdebt.treas.gov

PHONE: 1-800-943-6864
Offers online bidding for TreasuryDirect clients. Extensive data and research.

BONDS ONLINE

URL: www.bondsonline.com

PHONE: 1-817-885-8900
Basic resource links, news, and database of recent offerings. No trading facility.

BONDS2GO.COM

URL: www.bonds2go.com

PHONE: 1-888-577-4380
Industry professionals and institutional clients *only*. Affiliated with Century Securities Associates.

MUTUAL FUNDS

Choosing a mutual fund is a difficult task, since funds outnumber stocks on the NYSE. Also, a single fund may offer four or more versions (with identity letters such as A, B, C, and X), each carrying a different set of fees and sales loads. Online trading only increases the way those fees are calculated.

Each of the 10 largest no-load mutual funds offers online trading:

Fidelity	www.fidelity.com
Vanguard	www.vanguard.com
TIAA-CREF	www.tiaa.org
Dreyfus	www.dreyfus.com
Scudder	www.wscudder.com
T. Rowe Price	www.troweprice.com
Charles Schwab	www.schwab.com
American Century	www.americancentury.com
Strong Funds	www.strongfunds.com
E*Fund	www.e*fund.com

In addition, many of the trading sites listed in this directory offer a large inventory of no-loads, some including the above-mentioned funds. Again, check closely as to whether a representative is necessary to complete your transaction.

For help in simplifying cost comparisons, go to Morningstar at www.morningstar.net for an easy-to-use share class calculator. It will help you create a graph displaying the expected value over time of each share class available. The SEC requires a manual entry of fees and sales loads, as well as other information.

For example, if you're going to buy a load fund, you can find out how much that's going to cost over 25 years. The calculator lets you see all the share class data for one fund at once. It does take Java to run the applet, and the calculator graphics can be difficult to read. Still, Morningstar has the goods on every mutual fund in the world.

The SEC (www.sec.gov) also provides this information, but not in the comprehensive format offered by Morningstar.

COMMODITIES

Commodity trading is inherently stressful, and it will be interesting to observe its evolution on the Internet. Nonetheless, several sites are already devoted to providing online and/or discount commodity trades. Whether it's the so-called spot market or futures and options, trading can now be done with the click of a mouse.

A dealer can enter into a contract, agree to deliver a commodity at an agreed price, and take a short position—or enter into a contract, agree to accept the commodity, and pay the agreed price on delivery, taking a long position. Or the dealer can turn around and sell the commodity at a certain price at a certain time in the future in order to guard against the risks of adverse price changes.

Buyers, similarly, can contract to buy a commodity at a certain price at some time in the future in order to protect themselves against the risks of future adverse price changes. Between the buyers and the producers using futures to hedge and minimize risks are the speculators, or traders. They are buying and selling futures in the hope of earning a windfall profit by taking risks in the future price changes.

Many futures contracts take the form of options that are used to hedge against uncertainty about future prices. An option offers the right to sell or buy a commodity or stock at an agreed price within some specified future time. Once the option has been purchased, it can be exercised at the discretion of the option holder.

Here are four premier sites to investigate.

EXCEL TRADING GROUP

URL: www.xltrading.com

PHONE: 1-800-341-6942

Excel Trading Group is a division of LFG, LLC, a full service, Chicago-based clearing firm and member of all major North American commodities exchanges. Excel provides discount accounts for self-directed traders through its proprietary 24-hour online trading system with the ability to place, review, change, and cancel futures and options orders, review transaction history, and view account balances, including P&L.

E COMMODITIES

URL: www.e-contracts.com

PHONE: 1-800-357-3030

E Commodities is a full service commodity futures brokerage for traditional and online/electronic trading. It is affiliated with Coquest Inc., a self-guaranteed introducing broker and commodity trading advisor, founded in Dallas, TX in 1990. E Com offers direct floor access (via direct "ring down" lines) to all exchanges, and "flash-fill" order reporting. Electronic order entry software (iTrade) allows traders to create orders and send them directly to the floors of the principal exchanges, with an Internet-based quote delivery system. Traders can also opt for full broker assistance.

Another offering is the Toro Premier Fund, LP—a limited partnership, directed by senior trader Dennis Weinmann—assembled for the purposes of trading commodity futures and options. The fund features both the Coquest Indices Trading Method (approximately 90%), and the Coquest Energy Trading Method (approximately 10%). The minimum investment for the fund is $10,000.

XPRESSTRADE, LLC

URL: www.xpresstrade.com

PHONE: 1-800-947-6228

XPRESSTRADE is registered with the National Futures Association as a guaranteed introducing broker and is affiliated with ADM Investor Services.

ESSEX TRADING GROUP, LTD.

URL: www.essextrading.com

PHONE: 1-800-726-2140

DDJ Brokerage Corporation, Inc. (dba Essex Trading Group, Ltd) is registered with the CFTC and the NFA as a commodity trading advisor. Es-

tablished in 1983, Essex develops trading software for futures and options, including Futures Pro, Option Pro, Eurotrader, Tradex 21, and the
Advanced Channel Entry (ACE) line of programs, utilized by many of
the trading sites in this book. The minimum account size is $100,000,
and the proprietary software is used.

CONCLUSION

Technology has given ordinary people complex investment tools, without good advice on how to use them or on how to evaluate their choices. And for those who aspire to day trade, the amount of *mis*information is staggering. The factors involved—live quotes, execution routing and speed, live trade confirmation, and the variety of fees charged—can greatly affect the profitability of the most astute online trader!

This book represents the investigative work that anyone desiring to trade online would need to do in order to make an intelligent choice as to where to open a trading account. It is assumed that the reader is already familiar with the basics of online investing and wants to go to just one source to compare online brokerage costs, features, and benefits. This book is without ratings or opinions about the sites.

As more and more new trading sites come online, the competition will cause continual upgrading of capabilities among existing sites. Sites described in this book may radically change their focus, rates, and/or level of service—just as your level of trading may change based on your experience and availability of time and resources.

The key is to gain understanding about how trades are executed, what affects the cost of a trade, the limitations of your own operating system, as well as how the Internet potentially aids or hinders your profitable trading. Through normal Internet channels, there is a time gap between what appears on the monitor and what is "real-time." Likewise, orders routed through this system suffer some delay before execution. You must consider the type, size, and frequency of trades you will be making most often in order to calculate a trading site's charges for true comparison purposes.

Take advantage of *test drives* with imaginary portfolios and trial subscriptions of software and resources to become comfortable before risking your own money. And, most important, keep abreast of changes in technology and continue learning!

Best of luck . . . and if all else fails—buy the Greens and sell the Reds!

Larry Chambers

About the Authors

Today, **Larry Chambers** writes for some of the top national investment advisors representing over $10 billion in asset classes, as well as for one of the nation's leading CPA firms. Chambers has been published by major publishing houses, including Irwin, McGraw-Hill, Random House, Times Mirror, Dow Jones, and John Wiley & Sons, as well as featured in hundreds of national investment trade magazines.

After attending the University of Utah, where he received bachelor's and master's degrees and was elected to Phi Kappa Phi honor society, Chambers joined E. F. Hutton. At E. F. Hutton, he gained experience in managed money consulting for over 500 private and institutional accounts, including pension and profit-sharing plans, foundations, state retirement funds, and university endowments. He achieved an outstanding track record, was named one of the top 20 brokers out of more than 5,000, and received numerous awards and acknowledgments.

Chambers was a member of the American Society of Journalists and Authors and the Society of American Business Editors and Writers, and he is on the advisory board for the *Journal of Investing,* an Institutional Investor publication.

Karen Johnson is an editor and staff writer for Larry Chambers. She has researched and edited a number of books in the financial securities industry, and edits for some of the top financial columnists in magazines such as *Financial Planning, On Wall Street,* and *Registered Representative.* She was an English and business major at UCLA.